What Went Wrong?

The Arabs in History
The Emergence of Modern Turkey
The Assassins
The Muslim Discovery of Europe
Semites and Anti-Semites
The Political Language of Islam
Race and Slavery in the Middle East
The Middle East
The Multiple Identities of the Middle East

What Went Wrong?

THE CLASH BETWEEN ISLAM AND MODERNITY
IN THE MIDDLE EAST

BERNARD LEWIS

Weidenfeld & Nicolson
LONDON

First published in Great Britain in 2002
by Weidenfeld & Nicolson

© 2002 Bernard Lewis

Third impression May 2002

A CIP catalogue record for this book
is available from the British Library.

ISBN 0 297 82929 7

Printed in Great Britain by
Butler & Tanner Ltd, Frome and London

Weidenfeld & Nicolson
The Orion Publishing Group Ltd
Orion House
5 Upper Saint Martin's Lane
London WC2H 9EA

Contents

Preface

This book was already in page proof when the terrorist attacks in New York and Washington took place on September 11, 2001. It does not therefore deal with them, nor with their immediate causes and after-effects. It is however related to these attacks, examining not what happened and what followed, but what went before—the longer sequence and larger pattern of events, ideas, and attitudes that preceded and in some measure produced them.

B.L.
Princeton, N.J.
October 15, 2001

What Went Wrong?

Introduction

What went wrong? For a long time people in the Islamic world, especially but not exclusively in the Middle East, have been asking this question. The content and formulation of the question, provoked primarily by their encounter with the West, vary greatly according to the circumstances, extent, and duration of that encounter and the events that first made them conscious, by comparison, that all was not well in their own society. But whatever the form and manner of the question and of the answers that it evokes, there is no mistaking the growing anguish, the mounting urgency, and of late the seething anger with which both question and answers are expressed.

There is indeed good reason for questioning and concern, even for anger. For many centuries the world of Islam was in the forefront of human civilization and achievement. In the Muslims' own perception, Islam itself was indeed coterminous with civilization, and beyond its borders there were only barbarians and infidels. This perception of self and other was enjoyed by most if not all other civilization—Greece, Rome, India, China, and one could add more recent examples.

In the era between the decline of antiquity and the dawn of modernity, that is, in the centuries designated in European history as medieval, the Islamic claim was not without justification. Muslims were of course aware that there were other, more or less civilized, societies on earth, in China, in India, in Christendom. But China was remote and little known; India was in process of subjugation and Islamization. Christendom had a certain special importance, in that it constituted the only serious rival to Islam as a world faith and a world power. But in the Muslim view, the faith was superseded by the final Islamic

3

revelation, and the power was being steadily overcome by the greater, divinely guided power of Islam.

For most medieval Muslims, Christendom meant, primarily, the Byzantine Empire, which gradually became smaller and weaker until its final disappearance with the Turkish conquest of Constantinople in 1453. The remoter lands of Europe were seen in much the same light as the remoter lands of Africa—as an outer darkness of barbarism and unbelief from which there was nothing to learn and little even to be imported, except slaves and raw materials. For both the northern and the southern barbarians, their best hope was to be incorporated in the empire of the caliphs, and thus attain the benefits of religion and civilization.

For the first thousand years or so after the advent of Islam, this seemed not unlikely, and Muslims made repeated attempts to accomplish it. In the course of the seventh century, Muslim armies advancing from Arabia conquered Syria, Palestine, Egypt, and North Africa, all until then part of Christendom, and most of the new recruits to Islam, west of Iran and Arabia, were indeed converts from Christianity. In the eighth century, from their bases in North Africa, Arab Muslim forces, now joined by Berber converts, conquered Spain and Portugal and invaded France; in the ninth century they conquered Sicily and invaded the Italian mainland. In 846 C.E. a naval expedition from Sicily even entered the River Tiber, and Arab forces sacked Ostia and Rome. This provoked the first attempts to organize an effective Christian counterattack. A subsequent series of campaigns to recover the Holy Land, known as the Crusades, ended in failure and expulsion.

In Europe, Christian arms were more successful. By the end of the eleventh century the Muslims had been expelled from Sicily, and in 1492, almost eight centuries after the first Muslim landing in Spain, the long struggle for the reconquest ended in victory, opening the way to a Christian invasion of Africa and Asia. But meanwhile there were other Muslim threats to European Christendom. In the East, between 1237 and 1240 C.E., the Tatars of the Golden Horde conquered Russia; in 1252 the Khan of the Golden Horde and his people were converted to Islam. Russia, with much of Eastern Europe, was subject to Muslim rule, and it was not until the late fifteenth century that the Russians finally freed their country from what they called

Fig. I-1   The Bosphorus with the Castles of Europe and Asia by Thomas Allum

"the Tatar yoke." In the meantime a third wave of Muslim attack had begun, that of the Ottoman Turks, who conquered Anatolia, captured the ancient Christian city of Constantinople, invaded and colonized the Balkan peninsula, and threatened the very heart of Europe, twice reaching as far as Vienna.

At the peak of Islamic power, there was only one civilization that was comparable in the level, quality, and variety of achievement; that was of course China. But Chinese civilization remained essentially local, limited to one region, East Asia, and to one racial group. It was exported to some degree, but only to neighboring and kindred peoples. Islam in contrast created a world civilization, polyethnic, multiracial, international, one might even say intercontinental.

For centuries the world view and self-view of Muslims seemed well grounded. Islam represented the greatest military power on earth—its armies, at the very same time, were invading Europe and Africa, India and China. It was the foremost economic power in the world, trading in a wide range of commodities through a far-flung network of commerce and communications in Asia, Europe, and Africa; importing slaves and gold from Africa, slaves and wool from Europe, and exchanging a variety of foodstuffs, materials, and manufactures with the civilized countries of Asia. It had achieved the highest level so far in human history in the arts and sciences of civilization. Inheriting the knowledge and skills of the ancient Middle East, of Greece and of Persia,* it added to them new and important innovations from outside, such as the use and manufacture of paper from China and decimal positional numbering from India. It is difficult to imagine modern literature or science without the one or the other. It was in the

---

*The name Persia in its various classical and modern European forms comes from *Pars*, the name of the southwestern province of Iran, along the shore of the Gulf. The Arabs, whose alphabet contains no equivalent to the letter "p," called it "Fars." In the way that Castilian became Spanish and Tuscan became Italian, so the dialect of Fars, known as Farsi, came to be accepted as the literary, standard, and ultimately national language. In the classical and Western world, the regional name was also applied to the whole country, but this never happened among the Persians, who have used the name Iran—the land of the Aryans—for millennia and formally adopted it as the official name of the country in 1935. In speaking of past centuries, I have retained the accepted Western name.

Islamic Middle East that Indian numbers were for the first time incorporated in the inherited body of mathematical learning. From the Middle East they were transmitted to the West, where they are still known as Arabic numerals, honoring not those who invented them but those who first brought them to Europe. To this rich inheritance scholars and scientists in the Islamic world added an immensely important contribution through their own observations, experiments, and ideas. In most of the arts and sciences of civilization, medieval Europe was a pupil and in a sense a dependent of the Islamic world, relying on Arabic versions even for many otherwise unknown Greek works.

And then, suddenly, the relationship changed. Even before the Renaissance, Europeans were beginning to make significant progress in the civilized arts. With the advent of the New Learning, they advanced by leaps and bounds, leaving the scientific and technological and eventually the cultural heritage of the Islamic world far behind them.

The Muslims for a long time remained unaware of this. The great translation movement that centuries earlier had brought many Greek, Persian, and Syriac works within the purview of Muslim and other Arabic readers had come to an end, and the new scientific literature of Europe was almost totally unknown to them. Until the late eighteenth century, only one medical book was translated into a Middle Eastern language—a sixteenth-century treatise on syphilis, presented to Sultan Mehmed IV in Turkish 1655.[1] Both the choice and the date are significant. This disease, reputedly of American origin, had come to the Islamic world from Europe and is indeed is still known in Arabic, Persian, Turkish, and other languages as "the Frankish disease." Obviously, it seemed both appropriate and legitimate to adopt a Frankish remedy for a Frankish disease. Apart from that, the Renaissance, the Reformation, the technological revolution passed virtually unnoticed in the lands of Islam, where they were still inclined to dismiss the denizens of the lands beyond the Western frontier as benighted barbarians, much inferior even to the more sophisticated Asian infidels to the east. These had useful skills and devices to impart; the Europeans had neither. It was a judgment that had for long been reasonably accurate. It was becoming dangerously out of date.

Usually the lessons of history are most perspicuously and unequivocally taught on the battlefield, but there may be some delay before the lesson is understood and applied. In Christendom the final defeat of the Moors in Spain in 1492 and the liberation of Russia from the rule of the Islamized Tatars were understandably seen as decisive victories. Like the Spaniards and Portuguese, the Russians too pursued their former masters into their homelands, but with far greater and more enduring success. With the conquest of Astrakhan in 1554, the Russians reached the shores of the Caspian Sea; in the following century, they reached the northern shore of the Black Sea, thus beginning the long process of conquest and colonization that incorporated vast Muslim lands in the Russian Empire.

But in the heartlands of Islam, these happenings on the remote frontiers of civilization seemed less important and were in any case overshadowed in Muslim eyes by such central and vastly more important victories as the ignominious eviction of the Crusaders from the Levant in the thirteenth century, the capture of Constantinople in 1453, and the triumphant march of the Turkish forces through the Balkans toward the surviving Christian imperial city of Vienna, in what seemed to be an irresistible advance of Islam and defeat of Christendom.

The Ottoman sultan, like his peer and rival the Holy Roman Emperor, was not without political rivals and sectarian challengers within his own religious world. Of the two, the sultan was the more successful in dealing with these challenges. At the turn of the fifteenth–sixteenth centuries, the Ottomans had two Muslim neighbors. The older of the two was the Mamluk sultanate of Egypt, with its capital in Cairo, ruling over all Syria and Palestine and, more important, over the holy places of Islam in western Arabia. The other was Persia, newly united by a new dynasty, with a new religious militancy. The founder of the dynasty, Shāh Ismā'īl Safavī (reigned 1501–1524), a Turkish-speaking Shi'ite from Azerbaijan, brought all the lands of Iran under a single ruler for the first time since the Arab conquest in the seventh century. A religious leader as well as—perhaps more than—a political and military ruler, he made Shi'ism the official religion of the state, and thus differentiated the Muslim realm of Iran sharply from its Sunni neighbors on both sides; to the East, in Central Asia and India, and to the West, in the Ottoman Empire.

For a while, he and his successors, the shahs of the Safavid line, challenged the claim of the Ottoman sultans to both political supremacy and religious leadership. The Ottoman Sultan Selim I, known as "the Grim," who reigned from 1512 to 1520, launched military campaigns against both neighbors. He achieved a substantial but incomplete success against the Shah, a total and final victory over the Mamluk sultan of Egypt. Egypt and its dependencies were incorporated in the Ottoman realms; Persia remained a separate, rival, and for the most part hostile state. Busbecq, the imperial ambassador in Istanbul, went so far as to say that it was only the threat from Persia that saved Europe from imminent conquest by the Turks. "On [the Turks'] side are the resources of a mighty empire, strength unimpaired, habituation to victory, endurance of toil, unity, discipline, frugality, and watchfulness. On our side is public poverty, private luxury, impaired strength, broken spirit, lack of endurance and training; the soldiers are insubordinate, the officers avaricious; there is contempt for discipline; licence, recklessness, drunkenness, and debauchery are rife; and worst of all, the enemy is accustomed to victory, and we to defeat. Can we doubt what the result will be? Persia alone interposes in our favour; for the enemy, as he hastens to attack, must keep an eye on this menace in his rear. But Persia is only delaying our fate; it cannot save us. When the Turks have settled with Persia, they will fly at our throats supported by the might of the whole East; how unprepared we are I dare not say!"[2] There have been more recent Western observers who spoke of the Soviet Union and China in similar terms, and proved equally mistaken.

Busbecq's fears, as it turned out, were unjustified. The Ottomans and the Persians continued to fight each other until the nineteenth century, by which time they no longer constituted a threat to anyone but their own subjects. At the time, the idea of a possible anti-Ottoman alliance between Christendom and Persia was occasionally mooted, but to little effect. In 1523, Shāh Ismā'īl, still smarting after his defeat, sent a letter to the Emperor Charles V expressing surprise that the European powers were fighting each other instead of joining forces against the Ottomans. The appeal fell on deaf ears and the emperor did not send a reply to Shāh Ismā'īl until 1529, by which time the shah had been dead for five years.

Figure I-2
Wall painting in Isfahan, showing European visitors.
From the Chihil Sutun (Forty Columns) pavilions in Isfahan,
late sixteenth century, rebuilt 1706.

For the time being, Persia was immobilized, and under Selim's successor, Süleyman the Magnificent (reigned 1520–1566), the Ottomans were able to embark on a new phase of expansion in Europe. The great battle of Mohacs in Hungary, in August 1526, gave the Turks a decisive victory, and opened the way to the first siege of Vienna in 1529. The failure to capture Vienna on that occasion was seen on both sides as a delay, not a defeat, and opened a long struggle for mastery in the heart of Europe.

Here and there the Christian powers managed to achieve some successes, and one notable victory, the great naval battle of Lepanto, in the Gulf of Patras in Greece, in 1571. In Europe, indeed, this was acclaimed as a major triumph. All Christendom exulted in this victory, and King James VI of Scotland, later James I of England, was even moved to compose a long and ecstatic poem in celebration.[3] The Turkish archives preserve the report of the Kapudan Pasha, the senior officer commanding the fleet, whose account of the battle of Lepanto is just two lines: "The fleet of the divinely guided Empire encountered the fleet of the wretched infidels, and the will of Allah turned the other way."[4] As a military report, this may be somewhat lacking in detail, but not in frankness. In Ottoman histories, the battle is known simply as *Sıngın*, a Turkish word meaning a rout or crushing defeat.

But how much difference did Lepanto make? The answer must be very little. If we look at the larger question of naval power, let alone the far more important question of military power in the region, Lepanto was no more than a minor setback for the Ottomans, quickly made good. The situation is well-reflected in a conversation reported by an Ottoman chronicler, who tells us that when Sultan Selim II asked the Grand Vizier Sokollu Mehmed Pasha about the cost of rebuilding the fleet after its destruction at Lepanto, the Vizier replied: "The might and wealth of our Empire are such, that if we desired to equip the entire fleet with silver anchors, silken rigging, and satin sails, we could do it."[5] This is obviously a poetic exaggeration, but a fairly accurate reflection of the real significance of Lepanto—a great shot in the arm in the West, a minor ripple in the East. The major threat remained. In the seventeenth century, there was still Turkish pashas ruling in Budapest and Belgrade, and Barbary Corsairs from North Africa were raiding the coasts of England and Ireland and even, in 1627, Iceland, bringing back human booty for sale in the slave-markets of Algiers.

In the late sixteenth and early seventeenth centuries Persia once again became a factor of importance in the struggle. Shāh 'Abbās I, known as the Great, was in many ways the most successful ruler of his line. In 1598, returning to his capital after a victory against the Uzbeks of Central Asia, he was approached by a group of Europeans led by two English brothers, Sir Anthony and Sir Robert Sherley. Probably at their suggestion, he sent letters of friendship to the Pope, the Holy Roman Emperor, and various European monarchs and rulers, including the Queen of England and the Doge of Venice. These missives produced little result. Of greater importance was a reorganization and reequipment of his armed forces, undertaken with the Sherleys' and other Europeans' help. Between 1602 and 1612, and again between 1616 and 1627, Persia and Turkey were at war, and the Persians won a number of successes. Distracted by this struggle in the East, the Turks were obliged, in 1606, to make peace with the Austrians.

The Treaty of Sitvatorok, signed in that year, is notable for a number of reasons. All previous treaties had been dictated by the Turks in their capital, Istanbul. This one was negotiated on neutral ground, on an island in the Danube between the two sides. Perhaps even more significant was the recognition of the Emperor as "Padishah." Until then it had been the normal practice of the Ottomans to designate European rulers either by subordinate Ottoman titles such as *bey*, or more commonly by what they thought to be European titles. Thus, for example, Ottoman letters to Queen Elizabeth addressed her as "Queen (*Kıraliçe*) of the Vilayet of England," while the Emperor was addressed as "King (*Kıral*) of Vienna."[6] *Kıral* and *Kıraliçe* are of course terms of European, not Turkish origin, and were used by Ottomans in much the same way as imperial Britain used native titles for native princes in India. Addressing the emperor as "Padishah," the title that the Ottoman sultans themselves used, was a formal recognition of equality.[7]

While generally contemptuous of the infidel West, Muslims were not unaware of Western skills in weaponry and warfare. The initial successes of the Crusaders in the Levant impressed upon Muslim war departments that in some areas at least Western arms were superior, and the inference was quickly drawn and applied. Western prisoners of war were set to work building fortifications; Western mercenaries and adventurers were employed, and a traffic in arms and other war materials began that grew steadily in the course of the centuries. Even when the Ottoman Turks were advancing into southeastern Europe, they were always able to buy much needed equipment for their fleets and armies from Christian European suppliers, to recruit European experts, and even to obtain financial cover from Christian European banks. What is nowadays known as "constructive engagement" has a long history.

All this, however, had little or no influence on Muslim perceptions and attitudes, as long as Muslim armies continued to be victorious in the heartlands. The sultans bought war materials and military expertise for cash, and saw in this no more than a business transaction. The Turks in particular adopted such European inventions as handguns and artillery and used them to great effect, without thereby modifying their view of the barbarian infidels from whom they acquired these weapons.

There were some dissenting voices. As early as the sixteenth century, an Ottoman Grand Vizier in his retirement observed that while the Muslim forces were supreme on the land, the infidels were getting stronger on the sea. "We must overcome them."[8] His message received little attention. In the early seventeenth century another Ottoman official noted an alarming presence of Portuguese, Dutch, and English merchant shipping in Asian waters, and warned of a possible danger from that source.[9]

The danger was real, and growing. When the Portuguese navigator Vasco da Gama sailed round Africa into the Indian Ocean at the end of the fifteenth century, he opened a new sea route between Europe and Asia, with far-reaching consequences for the Middle East, first commercial, later also strategic. As early as 1502, the Republic of Venice, the prime European beneficiary of the eastern spice trade, sent an emissary to Cairo to warn the sultan of Egypt of the danger that this new sea route presented to their commerce. At first, the sultan paid little attention, but a sharp decline in his customs revenues focused his attention more sharply on this new problem. Egyptian naval expeditions against the Portuguese in eastern waters were however unsuccessful and no doubt contributed to the defeat of the Egyptian sultanate in 1516–1517 and the incorporation of all its dominions in the Ottoman realm.

The Ottomans now took over this task, but fared little better. Their efforts to counter the Portuguese in the Horn of Africa and the Red Sea were at best inconclusive. The lack of Ottoman interest in these developments is best illustrated by the response to an appeal for help from Atjeh, in Sumatra. In 1563 the Muslim ruler of Atjeh sent an embassy to Istanbul asking for help against the Portuguese and adding, as an inducement, that several of the non-Muslim rulers of the region had agreed to turn Muslim if the Ottomans would come to their aid. But the Ottomans were busy with more urgent matters—the sieges of Malta and of Szigetvar in Hungary, the death of Sultan Süleyman the Magnificent. After two years delay they finally assembled a fleet of 19 galleys and some other ships carrying weapons and supplies, to help the beleaguered Atjehnese.

Most of the ships, however, never got there. The greater part of the expedition was diverted to the more urgent task of restoring and extending Ottoman authority in the Yemen, and in fact only two ships, carrying gun founders, gunners, and engineers as well as some guns and other war material, actually reached Atjeh, where they were taken into the service of the local ruler and used in his unsuccessful attempts to expel the Portuguese. The incident seems to have passed unnoticed at the time and is known only from documents in the Turkish archives.[10] Whether through negligence or design, the Ottomans were probably fortunate in not challenging the Portuguese naval power in the eastern seas; their fleet of Mediterranean-style galleys would have fared badly against the Portuguese carracks and galleons, built for the Atlantic, and therefore bigger, heavier, better armed, and more maneuverable.

The impact of the new open ocean route between Europe and Asia on the transit commerce of the Middle East was less than was at one time thought. Throughout the sixteenth century, the Middle Eastern transit trade in spices and other commodities between South and Southeast Asia on the one hand and Mediterranean Europe on the other continued to flourish. But in the seventeenth century a new and—for the Middle East—far more dangerous situation arose. By that time Portuguese, Dutch, and other Europeans in Asia were no longer there simply as merchants. They were establishing bases that in time became colonial dependencies. As their power was extended from the sea to the seaports and even to the interior, the new European empires in Asia, controlling the points both of arrival and of departure in East–West commerce, effectively outflanked the Middle East.

The danger was not confined to West European expansion into South Asia. There was also the Russian expansion into North Asia where, again, Muslim rulers turned to the greatest Muslim power of the time, the Ottoman Empire, for help. There was some response. In 1568, the Ottomans drew up a plan to dig a canal through the isthmus of Suez from the Mediterranean to the Red Sea; the following year they actually began to dig a canal between the Don and Volga rivers. Their purpose, clearly, was to extend their naval power beyond the Mediterranean, on the one hand to the Red Sea and Indian Ocean, on the other to the Black Sea and the Caspian. But both operations, so it seems, were seen by the Ottomans as sideshows, and abandoned when they proved troublesome. By the end of the sixteenth century, the Ottomans withdrew from active participation on both fronts—against the Russians in North and Central Asia, against the West Europeans in South and Southeast Asia. Instead, they concentrated their main effort on the struggle in Europe that they saw, not without reason, as the principal battleground between Islam and Christendom, the rival faiths competing for the enlightenment—and mastery—of the world.

Western successes on the battlefield and on the high seas were accompanied by less resounding but more pervasive and ultimately more dangerous victories in the marketplace. The discovery and exploitation of the New World for the first time provided Christian Europe with ample supplies of gold and silver. The fertile lands of their new colonial possessions enabled them to grow new crops, including even such previous imports from the Middle East as coffee and sugar, and to export them to their former suppliers. The growing European presence in South and Southeast Asia accelerated and expanded this process, and old-established handicrafts faced the double challenge of Asian cheap labor and European commercial skills. The Western trading company, helped by its business-minded government, represented a new force in the Middle East. Here again an occasional voice expressed some concern but was little heeded.

Yet these developments and the accompanying changes in both internal and external affairs aggravated old problems and created new ones of increasing range and complexity—monetary, fiscal, financial, and eventually economic, social, and cultural.[11]

For most of the seventeenth century there were no major changes in the balance of military forces. Until almost the midcentury, Europe was absorbed in the Thirty Years War and its aftermath, while the Ottomans were preoccupied with problems at home and on their eastern frontier. A war with the Republic of Venice began in 1645, and at first went rather badly for the Turks. In 1656 the Venetians, who for some years had blockaded the Straits, were even able to send their fleet into the Dardanelles, and win a naval victory.

In that same year Mehmed Köprülü, an Albanian pasha, was appointed grand vizier. During his term of office (1656–1661) and that of his son and successor Ahmed Köprülü (1661–1678) the Ottoman state underwent a remarkable transformation. These skilled, energetic, and ruthless rulers were able to reorganize the armed forces of the Empire, stabilize its finances, and resume the struggle in Christian Europe. An area of intensive activity was Poland and the Ukraine, and it was here that, for the first time, the Ottomans came into conflict with Russia. By the Treaty of Radzin of 1681, the Turks gave up their claims on the Ukraine and agreed to give the Cossacks trading rights in the Black Sea. It was a portentous change, marking the emergence of a new and more dangerous enemy, and the beginning of a long, hard, and bitter struggle.

Meanwhile a new grand vizier had been appointed. Kara Mustafa Pasha was a brother-in-law of Mehmed Köprülü, and felt it his duty to restore the glory of the Köprülü vizierial dynasty. In 1682 he launched a new war against Austria, culminating in a second siege of Vienna, between July 17 and September 12, 1683. This second unsuccessful attempt to capture the city is best described in the words of the contemporary Ottoman chronicler Sılıhdar: "This was a calamitous defeat, so great that there has never been its like since the first appearance of the Ottoman state."[12] One must admire the frankness with which the Ottomans faced unpleasant realities.

The failure before Vienna was followed by a series of further de-feats. In 1686, with the loss of Buda, a century and a half of Ottoman rule in Hungary came to an end. The event is commemorated in a Turkish lament of the time:

In the fountains they no longer wash
In the mosques they no longer pray
The places that prospered are now desolate
The Austrian has taken our beautiful Buda.[13]

The retreat from Vienna opened new opportunities. In March 1684 Austria, Venice, Poland, Tuscany, and Malta, with the blessing of the Pope, formed a Holy League to fight the Ottoman Empire. Russia joined the Catholic powers in this enterprise. Under Czar Peter, known as the Great, they went to war against the Ottomans and achieved sig-nal successes. On August 6, 1696, Peter the Great captured Azov—the first Russian stronghold on the shore of the Black Sea.

By now the Turks were ready to discuss peace. The peace process began with secret negotiations between the Austrian chancellor and the newly-appointed Ottoman grand vizier, who—significantly—was accompanied by his grand dragoman, the Istanbul Greek Alexander Mavrokordato. In October 1698, the diplomats met at Carlowitz in the Voivodina, newly conquered by the Austrians from the Turks. Finally on January 26, 1699, with the help of British and Dutch me-diation, a peace treaty between the Ottoman Empire and the Holy League was signed at Carlowitz. A little later a separate agreement with the Russians confirmed the cession to them of Azov.

The Ottomans had suffered serious territorial losses. They had also been obliged to abandon old concepts and old ways of dealing with the outside world, and to learn a new science of diplomacy, negotiation, and mediation. The war was not a total defeat and the Treaty was not a total surrender. In the early eighteenth century they were even able to make some recovery. But even so the military result was unequivocal—the shattering defeat outside Vienna, the devastating loss of lives, stores, and equipment, and of course the cession of territory. The lesson was clear, and the Turks set to work to learn and apply it.

I

The Lessons of the Battlefield

The Treaty of Carlowitz has a special importance in the history of the Ottoman Empire, and even, more broadly, in the history of the Islamic world, as the first peace signed by a defeated Ottoman Empire with victorious Christian adversaries.

In a global perspective, this was not entirely new. There had been previous defeats of Islam by Christendom; the loss of Spain and Portugal, the rise of Russia, the growing European presence in South and Southeast Asia. But few observers at that time, Muslim or Western, could command a global perspective. In the perspective of the Muslim heartlands in the Middle East, these events were remote and peripheral, barely affecting the balance of power between the Islamic and Christian worlds in the long struggle that had been going on between them since the advent of Islam in the seventh century and the irruption of the Muslim armies from Arabia into the then Christian lands of Syria, Palestine, Egypt, North Africa, and, for a while, Southern Europe. The Crusaders had briefly halted the triumphal march of Islam, but they had been held, defeated, and ejected. The Muslim advance had continued with the extinction of Byzantium and the Ottoman entry into Europe. The Empire of Constantinople had fallen; the Holy Roman Empire was next. Ottoman and more broadly Muslim consciousness of the world in which they lived is reflected in the very copious historical literature that they produced and, in greater detail, in the millions of documents preserved in the Ottoman archives, illustrating the functioning of the Ottoman state year by year, almost day by day, in its manifold activities. There are occasional references to the loss of Spain, but it appears as a relatively minor issue—far away, not threatening. There is some mention of the arrival of Muslim refugees and of Jewish refugees who came from Spain to the Ottoman lands, but little more.

The peace signed at Carlowitz drove home two lessons. The first was military, defeat by superior force. The second lesson, more complex, was diplomatic, and was learnt in the process of negotiation. In the early centuries of Ottoman experience, a treaty was a simple matter. The Ottoman government dictated its terms, and the defeated enemy accepted them. After the first siege of Vienna there was, for a while, some sort of negotiation, and even—a startling innovation—a concession to the kaiser of equal status with the sultan, but no conclusive result one way or the other. In negotiating the Treaty of Carlowitz, the Ottomans had, for the first time, to resort to that strange art we call diplomacy, by which they tried, through political means, to modify, or even to reduce the results of the military outcome. For the Ottoman officials this was a new task, one in which they had no experience: how to negotiate the best terms they could after a military defeat.

In this, they had some assistance, some guidance, from two foreign embassies in Istanbul, those of Britain and of the Netherlands. The Ottomans at first were unwilling to accept what they regarded as Christian interference, but they soon learned to recognize and make use of such help. The Western maritime and commercial states had no interest in the consolidation and extension of Austrian power and influence in Central and Eastern Europe, and thought it would be more to their advantage to have a weakened but surviving Ottoman Empire, in which their merchants could come and go at will. The British and Dutch emissaries managed to provide the Ottomans with some discreet help and advice, and were even able to take part in the negotiation of the peace treaty.

Western help was not limited to diplomacy. Military help—the supply of weapons, even the financing of purchases, were old and familiar, going back beyond the beginnings of the Ottoman state to the time of the Crusades. What was new was for the Ottomans to seek European help in training and equipping their forces, and to form alliances with European powers against other European powers.

In the first half of the eighteenth century, the struggle was indecisive, and even brought some gains for the Ottomans. In 1710 and 1711 they won a significant victory over the Russians who, by the Treaty of the Pruth (1711), were obliged to return the peninsula of Azov. But another war against Venice and then against Austria ended with another defeat and further territorial losses, specified in the Treaty of Passarowitz of 1718.

At about that time, we have an Ottoman document, recording, or to be more accurate purporting to record, a conversation between two officers, one a Christian, (not more precisely described), the other an Ottoman Muslim.[1] The purpose of the document is obviously propagandistic. It is, to my knowledge, the first Muslim document in which Muslim and Christian methods of warfare are compared, to the advantage of the latter, and the previously unthinkable suggestion is advanced that the true believers should follow the infidels in military organization and the conduct of warfare. The document laid great stress in particular on the Christian use of firepower, both cannon and muskets, and on the training and reorganizations of their forces, to make the most effective use of both. "The superior skill of the Austrian lies only in the use of the musket. They cannot face the sword."[2] The thrust of the argument was that it was no longer sufficient, as in the past, to adopt Western weapons. It was also necessary to adopt Western training, structures, and tactics for their effective use.

That was bad enough; even worse was that this adoption by the Ottomans—and later the Persians and other Muslim armies—did not produce the desired result. The military confrontation revealed in a dramatic form the root cause of the new imbalance. The problem was not, as was once argued, one of decline. The Ottoman state and armed forces were as effective as they had ever been, in traditional terms. In this as in much else, it was European invention and experiment that changed the balance of power between the two sides.

The course of modernization even in this limited sense was by no means easy. It was denounced, it was resisted, it was interrupted. The case for modernization was considerably weakened by one of the many wars between Turkey and Iran that ended in 1730 with a victory for the even less modernized Persians. This did not strengthen the case of the modernizers in Turkey.

For a while things went rather better in Europe. The growing rivalry between their two main enemies in the north, Austria and Russia, helped the Ottomans to recover some ground. But then a new disaster struck. Between 1768 and 1774 the Ottomans suffered a series of defeats at the hands of the Russians. The result was registered in the Treaty of Küçük Kaynarca[3] of 1774, which gave the Russians rights of navigation and indirectly of intervention within the Ottoman Empire. Of more immediate importance was the clause concerning the Crimea, previously an Ottoman dependency inhabited by Turkish-speaking Muslims. The sultan was now compelled to recognize the "independence" of the khans of the Crimea. As it soon became clear, this was a preliminary to the annexation of the Crimea by Russia, in 1783.

This was a bitter blow. The loss of Ottoman territories in Europe was hard but could be borne. These lands were relatively recent conquests, with predominantly Christian native populations, ruled by a minority of Ottoman soldiers and administrators. The Crimea was another matter; it was old Turkish Muslim territory dating back to the Middle Ages, and its loss was felt as part of the homeland. This was the first—but by no means the last—loss of Muslim lands and populations to Christian rule. It also marked the conclusive establishment of Russia as a major Black Sea power, posing a threat to the Ottoman and more broadly the Islamic lands, both on the European and the Caucasian shores.

Clearly, new measures were needed to meet these new threats, and some of them violated accepted Islamic norms. The leaders of the ulema, the doctors of the Holy Law, were therefore asked, and agreed, to authorize two basic changes. The first was to accept infidel teachers and give them Muslim pupils, an innovation of staggering magnitude in a civilization that for more than a millennium had been accustomed to despise the outer infidels and barbarians as having nothing of any value to contribute, except perhaps themselves as raw material for incorporation in the domains of Islam and conversion to the faith of Islam.

The second change was to accept infidel allies in their wars against other infidels. The Ottomans were used to employing locally recruited Christian auxiliaries in their wars, and even contingents, whom they could treat as auxiliaries, from Christian powers with which they shared a common Christian enemy. The Ottoman records show that in addition to those of their Balkan subjects who embraced Islam, there were some who remained Christian and nevertheless served in auxiliary units attached to the Ottoman forces.

There were even gestures toward sovereign Christian states, who helped as what we would nowadays call allies, though neither side would have used such a term at the time. For example, in the correspondence between the Sultan of Turkey and Queen Elizabeth of England at the end of the sixteenth century, the letters are mostly concerned with commerce, but they do occasionally refer to the common Spanish enemy, a shared concern of London and Istanbul at the time. It would be an exaggeration to call this an alliance, and it was certainly not on equal terms. In the documents, the sultan, addressing the queen, uses language indicating that he expects her to be: ". . . loyal and firm-footed in the path of vassalage and obedience . . . and to manifest loyalty and subservience" to the Ottoman throne. The contemporary translation into Italian, which served as the medium of communication between Turks and Englishmen, simply renders this as *sincera amicizia*.[4] This kind of diplomatic mistranslation was for centuries the norm.

But the new relationship between the Ottoman state and its European friends as well as its European enemies was something quite different. By now it was clear that something was going wrong, and more and more people in the governing elite, and even outside the governing elite, were becoming aware of it. Even worse, they were beginning to be aware that Europe was doing better and that they were consequently weaker and more endangered.

When things go wrong in a society, in a way and to a degree that can no longer be denied or concealed, there are various questions that one can ask. A common one, particularly in continental Europe yesterday and in the Middle East today, is: "Who did this to us?" The answer to a question thus formulated is usually to place the blame on external or domestic scapegoats—foreigners abroad or minorities at home. The Ottomans, faced with the major crisis in their history, asked a different question: "What did we do wrong?" The debate on these two questions began in Turkey immediately after the signing of the Treaty of Carlowitz; it resumed with a new urgency after Küçük Kaynarca. In a sense it is still going on today.

Debates about what is wrong were not new. There was a long tradition of Ottoman memorialists, most of them members of the official bureaucracy, discussing the various domestic problems of the Ottoman state and society, suggesting causes, and proposing remedies. One such was a little book written by Lûtfi Pasha, grand vizier of Süleyman the Magnificent, after his dismissal from office in 1541.[5] In it he offered some acute diagnoses of flaws in the Ottoman structure and remedies that he thought should be adopted. Another was by a civil servant of Balkan origin called Koçu Bey, who in 1630 drew attention to weaknesses in both the civilian and the military services of the state, and proposed reforms to deal with them.[6] The basic fault, according to most of these memoranda, was falling away from the good old ways, Islamic and Ottoman; the basic remedy was a return to them. This diagnosis and prescription still command wide acceptance in the Middle East.

But these memoranda were relatively calm in tone and primarily domestic in content. They do occasionally refer to the outside world. Lûtfi Pasha, for example, drew attention to the importance of sea power. The Ottomans, he says, are everywhere triumphant on the land, but the infidels are superior at sea, and this could be dangerous.[7] He was right of course in this. It was European ships, built to weather the Atlantic gales, that enabled the west Europeans to overcome local resistance and establish naval supremacy in the Arabian and Indian Seas. By the eighteenth century, even Muslim pilgrims going from India and Indonesia to the holy cities in Arabia would often book passage on English, Dutch, and Portuguese ships, because it was quicker, cheaper, and safer.

But the rise of Europe was marginal to the concerns of Lûtfi Pasha and the other early memorialists, primarily concerned with domestic

Figure 1-1
Venetians bombard Tenedos. From a seventeenth-century
Turkish album, prepared for a European ambassador.

and, in the main, administrative and financial matters. The new memoranda, after Carlowitz, are more specific, more practical, more urgent, and more explicitly military. Also, for the first time, they make comparisons between the Islamic Ottoman Empire and its Christian enemies to the advantage of the latter. In other words, the question now was not only "what are we doing wrong?" but also "what are they doing right?" And of course, the essential question: "How do we catch up with them, and resume our rightful primacy?"

An important factor in the development of these new perceptions and in the literature in which they are expressed was travel—the reports and recommendations of travelers between the two worlds of Islam and Christendom. There had always been Western travelers in the East. They came as pilgrims visiting the Christian holy places; as merchants profiting, by permission of the Sultans, from the rich Eastern trade; as diplomats, serving in the embassies and consulates established by the European powers in Muslim capitals and provincial cities. There were also captives taken on the battlefield or at sea. Some of these Western visitors entered the service of Muslim governments. In the Western perspective they were adventurers and renegades; for the Muslims they were *muhtadi*, those who have found and followed the true path.[8]

The eighteenth century brought an entirely new category of Western visitors, whom we might describe in modern parlance as "experts." Some came as individuals to offer their services to Ottoman employers. Later, some were even seconded by their governments, as part of an increasingly popular type of arrangement between a Christian or post-Christian country on the one hand and the Ottoman or some other Muslim state on the other. Such arrangements continue to the present day. For Muslims, first in Turkey and later elsewhere, this brought a shocking new idea—that one might learn from the previously despised infidel.

An even more shocking innovation was travel from East to West. Previously only captives and a very limited number of special diplomatic envoys had gone that way. Muslims had no holy places in Europe to visit as pilgrims, as Christians visited the Holy Land. There was not much to attract merchants in a Europe that, for many centuries, was still a relatively primitive place with little to offer. The most valued commodity brought from Europe to the East was slaves, and these were usually supplied by Muslim raiders or European merchants.

Muslims were no strangers to travel. The pilgrimage to Mecca was one of the five basic obligations of the faith, and required Muslims, at least once in a lifetime, to make the necessary journey however long it might be. Muslims also traveled extensively in the countries to the south and to the east of the realms of Islam, in search of merchandise or knowledge. The lands and peoples beyond the northwestern frontier of Islam had little to offer of either, and such travel was in fact actively discouraged by the doctors of the Holy Law. Western captives in the East who escaped or were ransomed and returned home produced a considerable literature telling of their adventures, of the lands they had seen and the people they had met in the mysterious Orient. Middle Eastern captives in the West who found their way home for the most part remained silent, nor was there any great interest in the few accounts that survived. The Occident remained even more mysterious than the Orient, and it aroused no equivalent curiosity. The different mutual perceptions were vividly expressed in their attitudes to each other's languages. The study of Eastern languages was intensively pursued in the European universities and elsewhere by scholars who came to be known as Orientalists, on the analogy of Hellenists and Latinists. Until a comparatively recent date, there were no Occidentalists in the Orient.

The European powers had long followed the practice of maintaining permanent resident embassies and consulates, in the Islamic lands as elsewhere. The Islamic governments did not. It was the normal practice of Muslim sovereigns to send an ambassador to a foreign ruler when there was something to say, and to bring him home when he had said it. This eminently sensible and economical practice was maintained for centuries. Until the eighteenth century, there were very few such missions, and very few indications survive of what they reported.

In the eighteenth century the situation changed dramatically. Great numbers of such special envoys were now sent, with instructions to observe and to learn and, more particularly, to report on anything that might be useful to the Muslim state in coping with its difficulties and confronting its enemies. Several of the Ottoman ambassadors wrote reports, which clearly had a considerable impact at the time.[9] Among them were Mehmet Efendi who went to Paris in 1721; Resmi Efendi who went to Vienna in 1757 and to Berlin in 1773; Vasif Efendi who was in Madrid from 1787 to 1789; Azmi Efendi who was in Berlin from 1790 to 1792 and wrote an interesting memorandum on how a well-ordered state is governed and administered; and in many ways most important of all, Ebu Bekir Ratib Efendi,[10] who was in Vienna from 1791 to 1792 and described the system of civil and military government in the Austrian Empire in great detail, with specific recommendations concerning those practices that might usefully be copied.

The mission of Ratib Efendi differs from those of his predecessors both in quantity and in quality. The staff who accompanied him to Vienna consisted of more than one hundred military and civil officials; he stayed in Vienna for 153 days; his report ran to 245 manuscript folios, ten times or more than ten times those of his predecessors, and it goes into immense detail, primarily on military matters, but also, to quite a considerable extent, on civil affairs. Ratib Efendi also took the trouble to provide himself with much needed help on the language side. In his report he mentions two people who had been particularly helpful to him. One was the son of "the Jewish financier Camondo," one of the small group of Ottoman sephardic Jews who were living in Austria; the other was the famous Mouradgea d'Ohsson, an Ottoman Armenian who had long served as translator to the Swedish embassy in Istanbul. In his retirement he had gone to live in Paris, but because of the Revolution had moved to Vienna. These two provided much more than simple translation. Ratib Efendi, in his report, tells of Mouradgea d'Ohsson's visits and long conversations with him, and notes that the Armenian's zeal for the Ottoman state was at least as great as his own.

The recourse to Vienna was less surprising than it might at first appear. Events in France were bringing an important change. For almost three centuries, the Ottoman sultans had seen the Hapsburgs as their main enemies, and had looked to France and to a lesser extent to England for help against them. But the revolution in France created a new situation. The new sultan, Selim III (reigned 1789–1807), was clearly reluctant to drop the French connection, but the events in Paris obliged him to explore other possibilities—even the traditional enemy.

As well as embassy reports, there were also military memoranda. One of the earliest pieces of evidence, mentioned above, records an imaginary conversation between an Ottoman officer and a Christian officer, comparing their armies to the great disadvantage of the Ottomans. The purpose clearly was to prepare the Ottoman governing elite for drastic changes. This was bad enough in itself. That the changes should take the form of following Western practice was even more shocking. A major role in this process was played by European experts. Some of these came as individuals and threw in their lot completely with the Ottomans, to the point of embracing Islam and entering the Ottoman service. One such was a French nobleman, Claude-Alexandre, Comte de Bonneval, who arrived in about 1729, reorganized the bombardier force, and founded a "mathematical school" for the armed forces in 1734. He converted to Islam—allegedly to escape extradition on certain charges pending against him at home—and died in 1747. He is known in Turkish annals as Bombardier Ahmed (Humbaracı Ahmed).

Another famous convert was a Hungarian seminarist, probably Unitarian, known in Turkish annals as Ibrahim Müteferrika. Ibrahim's original family name is unknown; Müteferrika is a title, indicating membership of a kind of elite guard corps attached to the sultan's person. He seems to have arrived in the late seventeenth century and died in 1745. His major achievement was to establish a Turkish printing press in 1729.[11] One of the books he printed was a short treatise of his own, in which he explains the successes of Christian arms against the Ottomans in Europe and urges the need to reform Ottoman administrative and military procedures along European lines.[12]

As well as converts to Islam, there were a number of refugees who came from Europe, bringing useful skills. These included Christians whose beliefs were deemed heretical or schismatic in their countries of origin, and of course Jews. For a while in the late fifteenth and more especially in the sixteenth centuries, Jewish refugees from Europe played a minor but not unimportant role in Ottoman society—bringing European economic, technical, and medical skills, and occasionally serving in diplomatic missions. But with the cessation of Jewish immigration from Europe this virtually came to an end. Those who came from Europe had brought useful skills and knowledge; their locally-born descendants lacked these advantages, and their role was correspondingly diminished.

Of vastly greater importance were the Greeks. In the early years of Ottoman rule in the former Byzantine lands there was great bitterness among the orthodox Greeks at their treatment by the Catholic West, and the patriarch of Constantinople was famously quoted as saying: "Rather the turban of the Turk than the tiara of the Pope." But attitudes changed, and from the late seventeenth century it became customary for wealthy Greek families in the Turkish lands to send their sons to Europe, usually to Italy, for education. They particularly favored medical studies but also began to play an influential role as translators for the Ottoman government.

The office of interpreter to the Ottoman authorities was of course important in dealings with Europe. In earlier times it was held mostly by renegades and adventurers from the countries bordering the Ottoman Empire; Germans, Hungarians, Italians, and others. Later it was monopolized by Greek subjects of the Ottoman state who held the office and title of Grand Dragoman. The role of the Grand Dragoman Alexander Mavrokordato in the negotiation of the Treaty of Carlowitz was an important but by no means exceptional example. At this time, when the Ottomans sent an ambassador abroad he was invariably accompanied by a dragoman who was almost invariably Greek.

By the late eighteenth century the Ottoman state no longer needed to rely for its military reforms on renegades and adventurers, but could request and obtain the seconding of experts from European countries. One of the first and most important was the Baron de Tott, an officer of Hungarian origin in the French service who spent some time in Turkey in the 1770s, when he founded a new school of mathematics and contributed significantly to the training of the Ottoman forces in the new sciences of military engineering and artillery.[13] On his retirement in 1775, he was replaced as chief instructor by a Brit-

Figure 1-2
Engraving of the Kuleli Military School by Thomas Allom.
From R. Walsh, *Constantinople and the Scenery of the
Seven Churches of Asia Minor*, London, 1839.

ish officer, who later converted to Islam and who was known after his conversion as Ingiliz Mustafa. Since his original name was Campbell, his Turkish sobriquet seems doubly incongruous.

The dominant European influence however remained French, and most of the foreign instructors were either French or taught in the French language, the study of which was made compulsory for all students in the new military and naval schools. In 1789—a year of some significance in France—a new sultan, Selim III, ascended the throne of Osman. He had long been interested in reform, and had even corresponded, while still heir apparent, with the French King Louis XVI. He now embarked on an extensive program of military and administrative reform and reconstruction. At first the sultan, undeterred by the changes in France, turned to Paris for help; the Committee of Public Safety and later the Directoire responded. French-Ottoman cooperation was briefly interrupted by the Franco-Ottoman War of 1798 to 1802, but was later resumed, only to be interrupted again when Napoleon made peace with the czar at Turkish expense.

The Revolutionary and Napoleonic Wars, involving the whole of Europe, extended to Africa and more especially to Asia through the encounters there between the European colonial powers.

The relative weakness of the major Islamic powers had already in a sense been revealed by the first European expansion in Asia, when even small countries like Portugal and the Netherlands were able to establish themselves on the seas and on the coasts in defiance of the Muslim powers. The impotence of the Islamic world confronted with Europe was brought home in dramatic form in 1798, when a French expeditionary force commanded by a young general called Napoleon Bonaparte invaded, occupied, and governed Egypt. The lesson was harsh and clear—even a small European force could invade one of the heartlands of the Islamic empire and do so with impunity.

The second lesson came a few years later, when the French were forced to leave—not by the Egyptians nor by their Turkish suzerains, but by a squadron of the Royal Navy commanded by a young admiral called Horatio Nelson. This lesson too was clear; not only could a European power come and act at will, but only another European power could get them out.

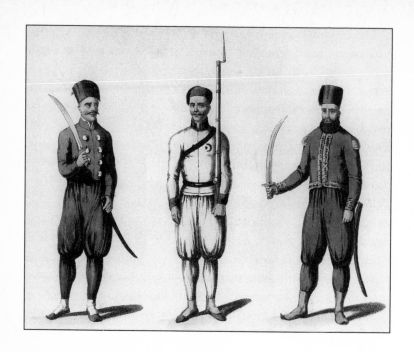

Figure 1-3
Western-style costumes of the New Troops.
From Charles MacFarlane, *Constantinople in 1828*,
Vol. II, London, 1829, frontispiece.

The message was repeated with new emphasis in 1807, and this time nearer home. Between 1806 and 1812 Turkey fought a major war against Russia. Britain was at first involved as an ally of Russia against Napoleon, and in February 1807 a British naval squadron commanded by Admiral Duckworth forced its way through the Dardanelles and threatened Istanbul. In this campaign the boot was on the other foot. While the sultan engaged the admiral in interminable negotiations, his men, directed by the French ambassador Sébastiani, rebuilt and strengthened the fortifications of the city so effectively that the British admiral was obliged to withdraw.

But in July of the same year Napoleon, to free himself for his war against England, made a deal with the czar at Tilsit, and was now ready to sacrifice Turkey to his new policy. The two emperors' plan for the partition of European Turkey gave the eastern Balkan provinces to Russia, the western Balkans to France, and assigned parts of Bosnia and Serbia to appease the Austrians. In the ensuing campaign the Russians crossed the Danube and by the Treaty of Bucharest of 1812 annexed Bessarabia, today known as Moldova, and acquired extensive rights in the Danubian principalities. Turkey, painfully, was learning the Great Game and, in time, gained some skill in playing it—enough to delay, though not to prevent, the final collapse of the Ottoman Empire.

Meanwhile a new force had arisen, which did much to accelerate and finally accomplish that collapse—the rise of the subject peoples within the Ottoman Empire. For many centuries, surprisingly to Western eyes, this was not a problem. The confrontation between Ottoman Islam and European Christendom has often been likened to the Cold War of the second half of the twentieth century. There are indeed some similarities between the two confrontations, but also significant differences. Perhaps most notable among these is the movement of refugees. In the twentieth century this movement was, overwhelmingly, from East to West; in the fifteenth, sixteenth, and even in the seventeenth centuries, it was primarily from West to East. Surely, the Ottomans did not offer equal rights to their subjects—a meaningless anachronism in the context of that time and place. They did however offer a degree of tolerance without precedent or parallel in Christian Europe. Each religious community—the Ottoman term was *millet*—was allowed the free practice of its religion. More remarkably, they had their own communal organizations, subject to the authority of their own religious chiefs, controlling their own education and social life, and enforcing their own laws, to the extent that they did not conflict with the basic laws of the Empire. While ultimate power—political and military—remained in Muslim hands, non-Muslims controlled much of the economy, and were even able to play a part of some importance in the political process.

The French Revolution, and the arrival of French troops and—more dangerous—French ideas in the Eastern Mediterranean brought a radical change. In February 1804, the Serbs launched their first national rising against the Ottomans, who dealt with it partly by suppression, partly by accommodation. In 1815, a second Serb rising was more successful and won them recognition as an autonomous principality under Ottoman suzerainty. The Greek uprising a few years later evoked widespread European support and achieved a sovereign independent Greek kingdom. In the course of the nineteenth and early twentieth centuries, the Christian peoples of the Balkans, one by one and step by step, freed themselves from Ottoman rule.

Iran, further from the main battlefields of Europe and lacking both opportunity and skill, was at this stage less able than the Turks to play the European powers against one another, and fared even worse. Here, too, the British, the French, and the Russians operated more or less at will, with the Russians taking the lion's share. By the Treaty of Gulistan of 1813, Iran ceded Derbent, Baku, Shirvan, Shaki, Karabagh and adjoining territories to Russia and renounced all claim to Georgia, Dagistan, and Mingrelia. A renewal of Russo-Turkish hostilities in 1825 was ended by the Treaty of Turkmanchay of 1828, by which Iran ceded the rest of Armenia to the Russians. The Russian advance against Islam was well under way, at the expense of Turkey, Iran, and the Central Asian states. It continued almost to our own day.

These wars starkly revealed the weakness of the Muslim states compared with the European powers. Military remedies for military failures were seen and understood to be inadequate. The quest for other causes and other cures began.

2

The Quest for Wealth and Power

Before the end of the eighteenth century Turks, Iranians, and other Middle Easterners had had very little opportunity for direct observation of the West—nothing remotely comparable with the opportunities that Westerners had enjoyed in the East even in the period when the West was inferior in every material and cultural respect. Contacts occurred mainly in three areas—diplomacy, commerce, and war. But while the European powers from relatively early times maintained offices, then consulates, and eventually embassies in the East, the Eastern powers did not follow this practice and sent only rare and brief special missions.

A similar disparity may be seen in commerce. Western merchants traveled extensively and, on the whole, freely in the Muslim lands. Middle-Eastern merchants did not normally travel in the West. Muslims had an extreme reluctance to venture into non-Muslim territory, and the Westerners did not want them to come. When, for example, it was proposed to establish an inn and warehouse for Turkish merchants in Venice, there was a long and anguished debate in the councils of the Venetian state, whether or not the Turks should be allowed to build such a center.[1] The importance of the Turkey trade for Venice was obvious, and Venetian merchants were well ensconced in Istanbul and other Turkish cities. But there were strong objections before the proposal was approved. One of the arguments was that this would be even worse than having Jews and Protestants, because unlike the Jews, the Turks had an army and a navy, and were therefore really dangerous. Sometimes, when the Turks sent one of their emissaries to a European ruler, there would be anxious debates in the country to which he was going, and even in the countries through which he would pass, on whether or not such envoys should be permitted to come or pass. This was by no means an easy or obvious question.

On the Muslim side, there was an equal reluctance to go to Europe. The Muslim jurists discuss at some length whether it is permissible for a Muslim to live in a non-Muslim country. They consider the case of the non-Muslim in his own country, or in their terms, the infidel in the land of the infidels, who sees the light and is converted to the true faith. May he stay where he is or may he not? The general consensus of the classical jurists is no. It is not possible for a Muslim to live a good Muslim life in an infidel land. He must leave home and go to some Muslim country. An even harder case was posed by the reconquest of Spain. If a Muslim land is conquered by the Christians, may they stay under Christian rule? The answer of many jurists was again no, they may not stay. The Moroccan al-Wansharīsī,[2] considering the case of Spain, posed what turned out to be a purely hypothetical question: if the Christian government is tolerant and allows them to practice their religion, may they then stay? His answer was that in that case it is all the more important for them to leave, because under a tolerant government, the danger of apostasy is greater.

The Muslim attitude was different from that of other eastern civilizations that suffered the impact of the expanding West. For Hindus, Buddhists, Confucians, and others, Christianity and Christendom were new and unknown. Those who came from there, and the things they brought, could therefore be considered more or less on their merits. For Muslims, Christianity, and therefore by implication everything associated with it, was known, familiar, and discounted. Christianity and Judaism were precursors of Islam, with holy books deriving from authentic revelations, but incomplete and corrupted by their unworthy custodians, and therefore superseded by the final and perfect revelation of Islam. What was true in Christianity was incorporated in Islam. What was not so incorporated was false.

On the Christian side there was a similar difference in attitude to the three major Asian civilizations, and for obvious reasons. Neither

Indians nor Chinese ruled the Christian holy land, nor had they conquered Spain, captured Constantinople, or besieged Vienna. Neither Hindus nor Buddhists nor yet Confucians had ever dismissed the Christian gospels as corrupt and outdated, and offered a later, better version of God's word to replace them. There were special difficulties in the long encounter between Islam and Christendom that were not present in the encounters between either of these civilizations and the remoter civilizations of Asia.

Muslims in general had little desire or incentive to venture into Christian Europe, and indeed the doctors of the Holy Law for the most part prohibited such journeys, except for a specific and limited purpose. The usual purpose—later the excuse—was to ransom captives. Some, but not all juristic authorities also permitted travel in infidel lands to purchase supplies in times of shortage.

Even among the very small number of people from Middle-Eastern countries who ventured into the West for diplomacy or commerce, a significant proportion were not Muslims but members of the minority religious communities. These were occasionally Jews, more often non-Catholic Christians, Greeks or Armenians, who were considered to be fairly reliable from an Ottoman point of view. Certainly they could not be suspected of sympathy with the Catholic powers.

In these circumstances it is not surprising that there was virtually no knowledge of Western languages. Only Italian had some currency in the Eastern Mediterranean, and served as a medium of communication between East and West. But even this involved Eastern Christians and Jews and rarely, if ever, Muslims. Minority doctors with Western training also played an increasing role in the practice of medicine. Arabic, Persian, and Turkish scientific writings of the period show some limited acquaintance with Western medicine and Western geography, both needed for practical reasons, but no awareness of Western history or culture.

The discovery of the New World illustrates both points. A Turkish version of Columbus's own (now lost) map, prepared in 1513, survives in the Topkapı Palace in Istanbul, where it remained, unconsulted and unknown, until it was discovered by a German scholar

Figure 2-1
Christopher Columbus at the Court of King Ferdinand.
Miniature from a Turkish manuscript of the *Tarih-i Hind-i Garbi*
(History of the West Indies), 1583–1584. Beyazid Library, Istanbul.
Courtesy of the Ministry of Culture of the Turkish Republic.

in 1929.[3] A Turkish book on the New World was written in the late sixteenth century, and was apparently based on information from European sources—oral rather than written. It describes the flora, fauna, and inhabitants of the New World, and, of course, expresses the hope that this blessed land would in due course be illuminated by the light of Islam and added to the sultan's realms. This too remained unknown until it was printed in Istanbul in 1729. [4]

An unwelcome import from the New World was syphilis, already reported in a Persian medical work by an author who died circa 1510.[5] This disease, which he calls "the Frankish pox," came, he said, from Europe, whence its name. It had already reached Azerbaijan before the end of the fifteenth century. In the prevailing view, the corpus of medical knowledge had reached perfection in the days of Avicenna, and in principle no change or addition was needed. Indeed, any change or addition was seen by some as impious. But syphilis was new, and came from Europe. It was therefore acceptable to translate European writings on the diagnosis and treatment of this disease. A collection of European writings was duly translated and presented to the sultan. Curiously, though the collection was presented in 1655, it consisted entirely of sixteenth-century European works.[6] Knowledge was something to be acquired, stored, if necessary bought, rather than grown or developed.

Middle Easterners, for practical purposes, had been willing to accept and use such Western devices as cannon and muskets, telescopes and eyeglasses. We have very good historical evidence about that. Under Muslim law, a man or woman has very little discretionary power to dispose of his or her property to heirs. Property had to be divided according to certain rules, which in the classical Ottoman Empire were strictly applied. There was a public official called a *Kassam*, whose duty was to see to the proper distribution of legacies amongst the heirs. For this purpose, the authorities had to prepare inventories and valuations. The central and provincial archives preserve hundreds of thousands of inventories of possessions of deceased persons, extending all over the empire and continuing for hundreds of years. These provide a priceless indication of the range and growth of what we might call practical Westernization, through the acquisition and possession of such Western products as clocks and watches, firearms, eyeglasses and telescopes, and even chairs. The figures of some eighteenth-century listings are revealing:

Clocks and watches	147
Pistols and muskets	76
Textiles	62
Chairs	57
Binoculars and telescopes	39
Glassware and flatware	38
Mirrors	33
Chests and drawers	21
Eyeglasses	12
Beds	5
Books and maps	5
Miscellaneous goods	5
TOTAL	500[7]

The process of conscious and deliberate modernization required, for the first time, closer and more sustained contact with Westerners, and obliged Middle Easterners in increasing numbers to learn previously despised European languages and even to endure periods of residence in European cities.

These visitors were of several kinds. The first were diplomats. The reforming Sultan Selim III decided, as part of his program of modernizing reforms, to adopt the European practice of continuous diplomacy through resident missions. His first was established in London in 1793 and was followed by others in Vienna, Berlin, St. Petersburg, and Paris.[8]

The problems and difficulties confronted by these first Middle-Eastern diplomats in Europe were in many respects the mirror image of those that had long faced their European counterparts in the East—how to perform their duties in a strange and alien society, nurtured on different scriptures and classics, inspired by different ideals and aspirations, and, to encapsulate them all, speaking a different and for most of them totally unknown language, written in an unknown script.

Figure 2-2
Mirza Abu'l Hassan Khan, Persian Ambassador to England,
painted by Thomas Lawrence in 1810. Courtesy of the Fogg Art Museum,
Harvard University Art Museums, Bequest of William M. Chadbourne.

Their position was much more difficult than that of the Europeans. These, as already noted, had a tradition of learning languages—scriptural, classical, and merely foreign. They had even been willing to undertake the study of more exotic languages. In the sixteenth and seventeenth centuries chairs of Arabic were established in the major European universities. Later Persian was added—but not Turkish. This being a modern language, it was, like English, French, German, et cetera, not seen as a subject for university study. But there were ample opportunities for Europeans to study Turkish outside the academic programs, and there was a considerable body of printed literature, in European languages, dealing with the history, culture, religion, and current conditions of the Islamic world. The European reader even had at his disposal a selection of Middle-Eastern classical literature in translation.[9] European Christians had a further advantage; they could also find help from the local communities of their Christian co-religionists, of whom there were many in Turkey, Egypt, Syria, and even as far east as Iraq and Iran. Except in North Africa, where Judaism lived on but Christianity died out, these communities continued to survive and even to flourish. An intense propaganda effort from Rome even persuaded significant segments of the Eastern churches to enter into communion with Rome, producing Uniate communities of Greek, Armenian, and Arabic speech. Muslim visitors had no comparable recourse in western Europe, where the Muslim communities had been expelled after the reconquest and where no contact or recruitment was permitted.

At first, Middle-Eastern diplomats in Europe found the same answer as their Western colleagues; to make use of dragomans who, initially employed as translators or interpreters, became far more than that, serving as intermediaries and sometimes as principals in major negotiations. The Turks in Europe, even more than the Europeans in Turkey, at first relied on these intermediaries. Much faster than their European colleagues, perhaps under far stronger compulsion, they made a determined effort to learn new languages and master new crafts.

They did so with astonishing speed and success. The first experiment in regular diplomatic relations launched by Selim III ran into difficulties and was abandoned. But a new start was made in the 1830s, and thereafter first Turks, then Persians, and then other Middle-Eastern governments, as these came into existence, attained a high level of diplomatic skill and professionalism.

At first their numbers were very limited, and Middle-Eastern governments soon became aware of the need for instruction in a variety of subjects and, more immediately, in the languages that provided access to these subjects. The practice therefore arose of sending students to study in Western countries.

It is difficult for a Westerner to appreciate the magnitude of this change, in a society accustomed to despise the infidel barbarians beyond the frontiers of civilization. Even traveling abroad was suspect; the idea of studying under infidel teachers was inconceivable.

The question of learning from infidels arose at a relatively early date in connection with directly military matters. The story is told in the Turkish chronicles of a Venetian war galley that was cast ashore in a storm and abandoned by its crew. Ottoman naval specialists examined the hulk, and found things that they thought it might be useful to adopt. But the religio-legal question arose—is it permissible to imitate the infidels? The answer of the religious authorities was that it is permissible to imitate the infidels in order to more effectively fight against them. The same argument was used in the eighteenth and early nineteenth centuries, when the ulema were again consulted on the lawfulness of the various Westernizing reforms in the armed forces and, more especially, the establishment of schools with European (not always converted) teachers and European (not always translated) textbooks. A question often asked by the memorialists was: "Why is it that in the past we were always able to catch up with the new devices of the infidels, and now we are no longer able to do so?" Interestingly, for a long time they did not ask why it was always the infidels who introduced the new devices. When they did ask this question, something more than modernization—catching up—was involved.

Adopting or copying infidel devices was one thing; learning from infidel teachers was another. Actually going to infidel countries to learn was an even more radical change. Nevertheless it had become necessary. First the pasha of Egypt, then the sultan of Turkey, then the shah of Persia all sent selected groups of students to London, Paris, and elsewhere. At first these student missions were overwhelmingly military, and their purpose was to ferret out and master the secrets of Western warfare. But this involved learning Western languages, and these students found other, perhaps more interesting, reading matter besides their military manuals. For the first time young Muslims from the Middle East were directly exposed to the impact of Western ideas. In the past, the barrier between the two civilizations was such that the Renaissance, the Reformation, and the scientific revolution had been irrelevant and unknown in the Islamic Middle East. But the revolutions in France offered new ideas and new models.

In earlier times, as a Turkish historian remarked, "the scientific current had broken against the dikes of literature and jurisprudence."[10] The enthusiastic and optimistic liberalism of the nineteenth century opened a sluice in the dike, through which first a trickle and then a flood of new ideas penetrated the hitherto closed Muslim elites.

One unexpected result of the impact of these new ideas was the appearance of a third category of Middle-Eastern visitors to the West—political refugees, those who had observed some Western practices, tried to apply them at home, and soon found it expedient to leave and go back, usually to London or Paris. But these too, after a period in exile, often returned home, sometimes as part of a change of regime and, more broadly, of outlook.

The new approach to language study brought a major change in communication and became a key factor in the relations between the civilizations. Contact with the West was no longer filtered through foreigners and minorities but was direct. This change became increasingly effective as ever larger numbers of Middle-Eastern Muslims were involved in the process. A turning point in the process of change occurred in 1821, with the outbreak of the Greek insurrection, which became the Greek War of Independence. The last of the Greek grand dragomans, Stavraki Aristarchi, was charged—probably unjustly—with complicity with the rebels, and executed. The Ottoman historians tell us that for a while incoming correspondence piled up in the office, with no one to read it. Then the problem was solved by bringing the chief instructor of the naval school, one Hoca Ishak Efendi, to take charge. Hoca Ishak Efendi (d. 1834) was a Greek Jew who converted to Islam and was a pioneer in the translation of Western scientific literature into Turkish—a task for which he had to create an entire new vocabulary.[11] After him the grand dragomans and their staffs were Muslims, and the Translation Office became a major ladder to influence and power. What mattered now was knowing how to talk to and deal with Europeans, knowing what was going on in Europe. Most of the major Ottoman statesmen of the mid- and late-nineteenth century rose by that ladder and not by the older ladders of the army, the bureaucracy, and the religious establishment.

The impact of the language revolution was not limited to classrooms and chanceries. Translation made Western books accessible to Middle-Eastern readers; another device of modernization, the printing press, made them more readily available.

With the crumbling of the language barrier direct observation of the West was now possible, and an increased recognition and more intimate awareness of European wealth and strength. The question now was more specific—what is the source of this wealth and strength, the talisman of Western success? Traditional answers to such a question would have been in religious terms. All problems are so to speak ultimately religious, and all final answers are therefore religious. The final answers given by traditional writers to the older formulation of the question were always "let us go back to our roots, to the good old ways, to the true faith, to the word of God." With that of course there was always the assumption that if things are going badly, we are being punished by God for having abandoned the true path.[12] That argument loses cogency when it is the infidels who are benefiting from the change.

Middle Easterners found it difficult to consider what we might call civilizational or cultural answers to this question. To preach a return to authentic, pristine Islam was one thing; to seek the answer in Christian ways or ideas was another—and, according to the notions of the time, self-evidently absurd. Muslims were accustomed to regard Christianity as an earlier, corrupted version of the true faith of which Islam was the final perfection. One does not go forward by going back-ward. There must therefore be some circumstance other than reli-gion or culture, which is part of religion, to account for the otherwise unaccountable superiority achieved by the Western world. A West-erner at the time—and many Muslims at the present day—might sug-gest science and the philosophy that sustains it. This view would not have occurred to those for whom philosophy was the handmaiden of theology and science merely a collection of pieces of knowledge and of devices. Muslims had their own philosophy that had retained and perfected the heritage of the ancients under the aegis of Islam. They had also their own science, handed down by their own great scientists of the past.

Instead they looked for the secret of Western success in those fea-tures of the West that were most distinctive, most different from any-thing in their own experience—and not tainted with Christianity. The French Revolution, the first major movement of ideas in Europe that was not explicitly or implicitly Christian, and even projected itself in the East as anti-Christian, had seemed for a while to offer such a choice. But under the Empire and the Restoration it lost this appeal. For the whole of the nineteenth and most of the twentieth century the search for the hidden talisman concentrated on two aspects of the West—economics and politics, or to put it differently, wealth and power.

The economy, and more especially industry, was seen as the prime source of wealth and therefore ultimately of military effectiveness. Halet Efendi, who was Ottoman ambassador in Paris from 1803 to 1806, observed: "If as an emergency measure once every three or four years, twenty-five thousand purses of aspers [a silver coin] were to be set aside and five factories for snuff, paper, crystal, cloth and porcelain as well as a school for languages and geography set up, then in the course of five years there will be as good as nothing left for them to hold onto, since the basis of all their current trade is in these five commodities."[13]

Halet's version is somewhat crude. Later rulers and ministers, first in Egypt, then Turkey, then other countries in the region, adopted more sophisticated versions of what was basically the same approach, and tried to catch up with Europe by building factories, principally to equip and clothe their armies. The effort failed, and most of the early factories became derelict.

Later attempts to catch up with the Industrial Revolution fared little better. Unlike the rising powers of Asia, most of which started from a lower economic base than the Middle East, the countries in the region still lag behind in investment, job creation, productivity, and therefore in exports and incomes. According to a World Bank estimate, the total exports of the Arab world other than fossil fuels amount to less than those of Finland, a country of five million inhabitants. Nor is much coming into the region by way of capital investment. On the contrary, wealthy Middle Easterners prefer to invest their capital abroad, in the developed world.

The other immediately visible difference between Islam and the West was in politics and more particularly in administration. Already in the eighteenth century ambassadors to Berlin and Vienna, later to Paris and London, describe—with wonderment and sometimes with admiration—the functioning of an efficient bureaucratic administration in which appointment and promotion are by merit and qualification rather than by patronage and favor, and recommend the adoption of something similar.

The impact of Western example and Western ideas also brought new definitions of identity and consequently new allegiances and aspirations. Two ideas were especially important, both new in a culture where identity was basically religious and allegiance normally dynastic. The first was that of patriotism, coming from Western Europe, particularly from France and England, and favored by the younger Ottoman elites, who saw in an Ottoman patriotism a way of binding together the heterogeneous populations of the empire in a common love of country expressed in a common allegiance to its ruler. The second, from Central and Eastern Europe, was nationalism, a more ethnic and linguistic definition of identity, the effect of which in the Ottoman political community was not to unify but to divide and disrupt.

The influence of Central- and East-European–style nationalism was vastly greater than that of West-European–style patriotism, and even where patriotism was adopted, it was given a national rather than an empire-wide content. European patterns of identity and allegiance were alien to the peoples of the Middle East, but not equally so. The situation in a fragmented Germany and Italy and in the polyglot Austrian and Russian empires was much closer to Middle-Eastern conditions, and the message that was brought—for example by Hungarian and Polish refugees—was much more readily intelligible. After the events of 1848 a number of Hungarian refugees went to Turkey, and many of them stayed. Some learned Turkish, some became Muslims, and their role in the development of these new ideas in Turkey is considerable. The same is true, though to a lesser extent, of Poles who also came to seek refuge.

These ideas had powerful and contradictory impacts on the attitudes and expectations of the Ottoman population and particularly the non-Muslim subject peoples. On the one hand, Ottoman patriotism and the new reforms appeared to offer them legal and civic equality with the previously dominant Muslims. At the same time nationalism inspired the desire for separate national sovereignty, free from what they were increasingly beginning to regard as the oppressive Ottoman yoke. Both undermined the old consensus, which had enabled people of many different faiths and nations to live together in reasonable harmony under the supreme authority of the sultan.

All this happened at a time when the non-Muslim subjects and more especially the Christians were thriving mightily. There were several causes for this. One was better education. For obvious reasons, they had better opportunities to learn languages, travel and receive Western schooling—the non-Muslims more than the Muslims, the Christians more than the Jews. For another, they enjoyed the patronage of the European powers. These again preferred non-Muslims to Muslims and Christians to Jews, in both respects reversing the traditional situation.

And of course, arising from these, the Ottoman Christians and Jews enjoyed the common minority advantage of their own networks of kinsfolk and co-religionists, especially abroad.

The Muslims on their side were still inhibited by their old disdain for the infidels and more particularly for traditional infidel occupa-

Figure 2-3

Cafes in Damascus. From *Syria, the Holy Land, Asia Minor, etc.* Illustrated by W.H. Bartlett, William Purse, etc., London, 1836.

tions. Certain professions and occupation were regarded as Jewish, Greek, or Armenian and therefore undignified for a Muslim or a Turk to follow. This sort of choice is not unfamiliar in other societies and other times. Perhaps for these reasons most of the state-sponsored economic enterprises were unsuccessful, while the minorities and their foreign patrons increasingly controlled the economy. At a certain stage one must rather say foreigners and their minority proteges.[14]

The changed relationship may be seen in a simple example, that traditional Middle-Eastern indulgence, a cup of coffee. Coffee originally came from Ethiopia. It was brought up both shores of the Red Sea, through Arabia and Egypt, to Syria and to Turkey, and then exported to Europe. Sugar came from Persia and India. For a long time, both coffee and sugar were imports to Europe, either through or from the Middle East. But then the colonial powers found that they could grow coffee and sugar more abundantly and more cheaply in their new colonies. They did this so thoroughly and successfully that they began to export coffee and sugar to the Ottoman lands. By the end of the eighteenth century, if a Turk or Arab took the traditional indulgence, a cup of sweetened coffee, in all probability the coffee came from Dutch Java or Spanish America, the sugar from the British or French West Indies; only the hot water was local. In the nineteenth and early twentieth centuries, even that ceased to be true, as European concessionary companies took over the water supply and gas supply in Middle Eastern cities.

In the meantime the process of modernization was accentuated and accelerated by three major developments in communication:

1. Printing. The establishment and spread of printing presses.
2. Translation. At first this was limited; then increasing numbers of books were translated, printed, and distributed in Turkish, Arabic, and Persian. The earliest translations obviously were of works deemed useful by the rulers and officials who commissioned them. But in time works of literary content were also translated and published.
3. Newspapers. The first were produced and distributed by foreigners. The French Embassy in Istanbul brought the message

of the Revolution in the *Gazette Française de Constantinople*, established in 1795 and addressed to the French-speaking community and of course to those who had learned to read French. Bonaparte in Egypt also established newspapers. Then came business interests, and in 1824 the first business-sponsored newspaper appeared in Izmir.

A significant contribution was made by Christian missions. Proselytizing Muslims was a capital offense, but the Ottoman authorities had no objection to Western Catholics and Protestants competing to win over the Eastern Christians to their rites. Religious propaganda in Greek and Armenian had little or no impact outside those communities. But the Christians of the Arabic-speaking countries used Arabic, and the newspapers and other literature produced for their benefit by the Jesuits in Beirut, later by other groups, gained a wider readership.

The earliest locally sponsored newspapers were governmental—the Egyptian *Gazette*, the Ottoman *Monitor*, and their equivalents elsewhere. An editorial in the first issue of the Ottoman *Monitor*, dated May 14, 1832, sets forth the purpose and functions of these early official newspapers. The newspaper, it explains, is a natural development of the old tradition of imperial historiography, with the same function of "making known the true nature of events and the real purport of the acts and commands of the government, in order to prevent misunderstanding and forestall uninformed criticism." This conception of the role of the press has not entirely disappeared from the region. "A further purpose," the article explains, "is to provide useful knowledge on commerce, science and the arts."[15]

Eventually a significant nonofficial local press developed in local languages—Turkish, Persian, Arabic. Its development was enormously helped by the introduction of another Western device, the telegraph, at the time of the Crimean War (1854–56). It is sadly appropriate that the first telegraphic message sent from the Middle East to the outside world was a military communiqué: "Sebastopol has fallen." It is also sadly appropriate in that it was inaccurate; it hadn't yet fallen. That didn't happen until a little later.

The telegraph brought enormous changes. It made possible the supply and dissemination of news, and also intelligence—through both public and private channels—in a manner unprecedented in the region. This was of immense advantage both to official and private reporting.

Along with the telegraph, the Crimean War brought another innovation—the war correspondent. Now for the first time West European journalists arrived in the Ottoman lands, with the task of providing regular reports to avid readers of daily newspapers in London, Paris, and elsewhere. Some of them also made arrangements to provide reports to local newspapers, and some of these in turn, for the first time, began to publish daily. It was a change of immense significance, and transformed Middle-Eastern peoples' perception both of themselves and of the world of which they were a part.

One example may suffice to illustrate the magnitude of the resulting change. One of the greatest of the Ottoman imperial historiographers, Naima (1655–1716), was responsible for covering the period from 1590 to 1660. The account of these 70 years occupies no less than six volumes, and goes into great detail on events in Central Europe and the different aspects of the struggle between the Austrian and Ottoman forces. The Thirty Years War—which one might have thought of some interest to the Turks—is dismissed in a couple of pages consisting mostly of a transcript of an earlier chronicle, which the imperial historiographer did not even bother to edit—for example, referring to Philip IV as "still King of Spain at the present time."[16] King Philip died in 1665, when Naima was ten years old. The contrast is all the more striking between this classical disdain of the outside world and the Turkish newspapers of the 1860s, which cover and discuss such matters as the American Civil War and the Polish insurrection of 1863–64. Finally the introduction of steamships, railways, and the building of a network of roads vastly accelerated communication, both with the outside world and within the region.

The establishment of newspapers and magazines in Arabic, Persian, and Turkish brought several significant changes—the opportunity, for the first time, to follow events inside and outside the Islamic world; the emergence of a new and more flexible language, with the conceptual and lexical resources to discuss these developments; and, in many ways most significant of all, the emergence of a new figure— the journalist.

Together with the journalist came another newcomer, whose appearance was equally portentous—the lawyer. In an Islamic state, there is in principle no law other than the sharī'a, the Holy Law of Islam. The reforms of the nineteenth century and the needs of commercial and other contacts with Europe led to the enactment of new laws, modeled on those of Europe—commercial, civil, criminal, and finally constitutional. In the traditional order the only lawyers were the ulema, the doctors of the Holy Law, at once jurists and theologians. The secular lawyer, pleading in courts administering secular law, represented a new and influential element in society.

Education too, in the old order, had been largely the preserve of the men of religion. This also was taken from them, as reforming and imperial rulers alike found it necessary to establish schools and later colleges and universities, to teach modern skills and dispense modern knowledge. The new-style teacher, sometimes schoolmaster, sometimes professor, joined the journalist and the lawyer as one of the intellectual pillars of the new order.

The cumulative effect of reform and modernization was, paradoxically, not to increase freedom but to reinforce autocracy:

1. By strengthening the central power through the new apparatus of communication and enforcement that modern technology placed at its disposal, and
2. By enfeebling or abrogating the limiting traditional intermediate powers such as the provincial gentry and magistracy, the urban patriciate, the ulema, and the old-established military bodies such as the Corps of Janissaries. Their authority derived from tradition and recognition rather than from the central government, toward which they could therefore afford to adopt a more independent attitude. During the seventeenth and eighteenth centuries their power, in the provinces and even in the capital,

had grown steadily at the expense of an increasingly weak central government. In the course of the nineteenth century these intermediate powers were either abolished, like the Corps of Janissaries, or brought under control.

Parenthetically it may be noted that the most recent effects of modernization, especially in communication, have tended in the opposite direction. Television and satellite, fax and internet, have brought and imposed a new openness, and are beginning to undermine the closed society and closed minds that sustain autocracy. Similarly the spread of education or at least of literacy to much larger elements of the population has again imposed new limits on the autocracy of rulers and—may I add?—of teachers.

But that came much later, in our own day. At the time of the nineteenth century reforms the effect of modernization was increased and reinforced autocracy, at once more effective and more visible. This focused the attention of Middle-Eastern seekers on another distinctively European practice, that of constitutional and representative democracy, sometimes called freedom.

These new perceptions brought about some changes in the traditional system of political values. Muslims have always given considerable attention to what in Western parlance might be classed as both political science and constitutional law. For Muslims, it was that part of the divinely ordained Holy Law that dealt with the role of the ruler and the relationship between him and the body of believers who constituted his subjects. Westerners have become accustomed to think of good and bad government in terms of tyranny versus liberty. In Middle-Eastern usage, liberty or freedom was a legal not a political term. It meant one who was not a slave, and unlike the West, Muslims did not use slavery and freedom as political metaphors. For traditional Muslims, the converse of tyranny was not liberty but justice. Justice in this context meant essentially two things, that the ruler was there by right and not by usurpation, and that he governed according to God's law, or at least according to recognizable moral and legal principles. The first of these raised important questions concerning succession, which became increasingly urgent after the abolition of most of the monarchies in the region. The second was sometimes discussed in terms of a contrast between arbitrary and consultative government. Both remain crucial issues at the present day.

In addition to the basic contrast between tyranny and justice there was a second contrast, often though not always invoked, between arbitrary and consultative government. The first denoted the capricious ruler deciding and acting on his own; the second the wise and just ruler who consulted others. While Muslim texts from the Qur'ān onward speak of "consultation," no formal procedure of consultation or definition of those to be consulted was ever worked out in theory, let alone applied in practice.

Words meaning "free" and "freedom," in a political sense, occur occasionally in eighteenth-century Middle-Eastern writings, always in a European context. An early-eighteenth-century Turkish treatise on the states and governments of Europe speaks of Danzig as a free city; a Turkish ambassador who went to France in 1720 was taken to see the "free cities" of Toulouse and Bordeaux, and explains in his report what this means. Each city, he says, was the seat of a *parlement* and *président*. Both words are given in French, transcribed in the Turco-Arabic script, and interpreted. The Ottoman Ambassador Azmi Efendi, who passed through Hungary in 1790 on his way to Berlin, noted that the previous Emperor Joseph had deprived the Hungarians of their "ancient freedoms," but that the Emperor Leopold had restored them.[17] Embassy reports from revolutionary Paris speak occasionally—usually negatively—of freedom, and the Chief Secretary Atif Efendi, in a memorandum written in 1798[18] to inform the Imperial Council in Istanbul of the political situation created by the Revolution in France and the propaganda conducted by the revolutionary government, uses the word a number of times. In the same year General Bonaparte, commanding the French expedition to Egypt, informed the Egyptians on his arrival that he had come on behalf of the French Republic, "founded on the basis of freedom and equality." Fraternity seems to have been lost in transit.

But the new ideas of freedom and participation, inspired by English practice and French theory, gradually found their way into the Middle East—first to the Christian subjects and minorities, more open to influences emanating from Christendom, eventually to the Muslim majority. Already in 1807 and 1808 groups of Ottoman subjects made two unprecedented attempts to define and demarcate the authority of the sultan and the notables in contractual documents. The Ottoman historian Şanizade, who died in 1826, makes some very significant observations in his account of the events of the year 1236/ 1820–21. In this passage he speaks with approval of the holding of "consultative meetings." He of course ascribes them to Islamic and Ottoman precedents, but at the same time he observes that such consultations are customary in "certain well-organized states," clearly a euphemism for the states of Europe. More remarkably, he attributes to the persons attending these meetings a role new to Islamic political thought and practice. The members of these councils, he notes, consist of two groups, the "servants of the state" and the "representatives of the subjects" (*vükela-i raiyyet*). They discuss and argue freely (*ber vech-i serbestiyet*) and thus reach a decision. In this underemphasized, almost imperceptible manner he introduces such new and strange notions as popular representation, free debate, and corporate decision.[19]

In the course of the nineteenth century the notion of political freedom became familiar in a number of ways—through translations of European books, reports and discussions of European affairs, and, after a while, through the influence of diplomats, students, and, later, refugees returning from Europe.

Before long, Middle-Eastern Muslims began to discuss the possible relevance of these ideas to their own situation. At first, their approach was cautious and conservative. Their concept of freedom owed much to the German idea of the *Rechtsstaat*, and could easily be presented as a development of the classical Islamic concept of justice. Similar ideas are expressed by several writers of the time, and underlie the great Ottoman Reform Edict of 1839 and its successors. They also inspired the reforming minister Mustafa Reşid Pasha, who stopped in Vienna in 1834 on his way to take up his appointment as ambassador in Paris. He is reported to have had a conversation with Prince Metternich.

An important figure in the introduction and dissemination of these ideas was Sadık Rıfat Pasha (1807–1856), who drafted a memorandum on reform while he was Ottoman ambassador in Vienna in 1837 and in close touch with Prince Metternich. Like most other Middle-Eastern visitors, Sadık Rıfat Pasha was greatly impressed by European progress and prosperity and saw in the adoption and adaptation of these the best means of regenerating his own country. European wealth, industry, and science, he explains, are the result of certain political conditions, ensuring stability and tranquillity. These in turn depend on "the attainment of complete security for the life, property, honor and reputation of each nation and people, that is to say, on the proper application of the necessary rights of freedom."[20]

But there were other more radical interpretations of freedom on offer in Paris and London, and as the screws of the new autocracy were tightened, these became increasingly attractive to young educated Muslims. This attraction was if anything increased rather than diminished by the spread of British and French domination in important parts of the Muslim world. This was, after all, another indication of the power that democracy gave them; moreover these new masters were willing to share at least the idea of freedom with their new subjects. Some, including such notable figures as Edmund Burke and Lord Macaulay, were willing to go much further and demand the extension of English freedom to England's colonial subjects.

In the Middle East some autocratic rulers made gestures—hardly more than that—in the direction of constitutional government. In 1861 the Bey of Tunis, an Ottoman dependency, proclaimed a constitution, with a grand council of 60 members, some appointed, some co-opted. It was suspended in 1864 with the establishment of the French Protectorate. In 1866 the Khedive of Egypt, another Ottoman dependency, convened a "consultative assembly of delegates," consisting of 75 delegates elected for a three-year term by a system of indirect, collegiate elections. To a large extent, these measures were not so much imitation as propitiation, not of their own subjects but of the European powers whose political pressure they feared and whose financial support they wanted. Unsurprisingly, these measures may have sharpened but did not satisfy the desire for greater freedom and participation.

In the mid-1860s a new movement was launched—the Young Ottomans. Even the use of the word "Young" is interesting. We have now become accustomed in the Western world to using "young" as a positive political term. In the Middle East in the nineteenth century this was new and strange. The connotation of "young" was inexperienced and immature, and no group would have thought of putting themselves forward for any kind of office on the basis of being young. On the contrary, all the terms of respect mean old, senior. The primary meaning of the Arabic *shaykh* and of the Persian *pir* is "old." Both carry a connotation of political or religious authority. The Turkish *aga* has the primary meaning of "elder brother." In some Turkic languages it means "father," "uncle," and even "elder sister." In Ottoman usage it connoted command or authority, military or other. The Aga of the Janissaries commanded that corps; the Aga of the Girls (*Kızlar agası*), the chief black eunuch of the imperial harem, maintained order in that institution. A similar respect for age—for seniority—appears in Western languages, in the common use of such words as "elder" and "alderman," "Senate," 'Senator," and "senior." It is interesting that both the Young Ottomans and their later successors, the Young Turks, avoided using the normal Turkish word for "young" in their nomenclature. The Young Ottomans called themselves *Yeni*, which literally means "new." The Young Turks called themselves *Jöntürk*, simply transliterating their French designation.

The Young Ottomans were obviously formed on the analogy of the Italian liberal patriot Giuseppe Mazzini's Young Italy and Young Europe; they agitated for a constitution and a parliament, with the inevitable result that in 1867 their leaders went into exile, mostly to London and Paris. They returned in 1870, and in 1876, with the help of some pressure from the European powers, they were able to persuade the sultan to proclaim a brand new constitution, providing for a parliament, with a nominated senate and a popularly elected chamber.

This constitution, which owed much to the example of the Belgian constitution and more to that of the Prussian constitutional enactment of 1850, was far from libertarian. Even so, it was too much. Two elections were held, the first in March 1877, the second, after a

Figure 2-4

Opening speech of the Ottoman Parliament at the Dolmabahçe Palace. From *Die Heutige Türkei*, Leipzig-Berlin, 1882.

forced dissolution, in December of the same year. The first Ottoman parliament sat for two sessions, of about five months in all. Nevertheless, the elected members showed considerable vigor, and no doubt for that reason on February 14, 1878 the sultan, exercising the imperial prerogative, summarily dismissed parliament. It did not meet again for 30 years.

In Egypt, the assembly first convened in 1866, met for its three prescribed terms, and was followed by other similar assemblies. After the British occupation in 1882, further steps were taken to provide a form of constitutional and parliamentary government, naturally with severely limited powers. But even these were greatly in excess of anything existing anywhere else in the Middle East. This imperialist-controlled enclave became a haven of refuge for political refugees from the independent lands, offering them a freedom of expression and discussion available nowhere else in the region. For a long time, "freedom" and "independence" were used as virtually synonymous terms. More recent experience has demonstrated that they are very different, and may even, in certain situations, be mutually exclusive.

A new phase began with the Russo-Japanese War of 1905 and with the Japanese victory, which was acclaimed all over Asia and Africa. At last an Eastern country had successfully defied and even defeated a European imperial power. There were some who drew a further lesson from this victory. Japan was the only Eastern power that had adopted a form of constitutional and parliamentary government. Russia was the only European power that had rejected it. The Japanese victory seemed to offer final proof of the proposition that constitutional democracy makes a nation healthy, wealthy, and strong.

Even among the defeated Russians there were constitutional stirrings. In the Middle East, two constitutional revolutions followed, first in Persia in 1906, then in Turkey in 1908. Both began with hope and enthusiasm. Both ended, after brief intervals, in even more despotic regimes, ruling even more impoverished and enfeebled countries.

By 1920, it seemed that the triumph of Europe over Islam was complete. In Afghanistan and inner Arabia and a few other places difficult of access and offering no attraction, independent Muslim rulers maintained the old ways. Otherwise, new rulers and new ways, introduced or imitated from Europe, prevailed everywhere. Even in the former Russian empire, riven by revolution and civil war, Moscow was reasserting its control over the former, briefly liberated, Muslim dominions of the tsars.

The once great Ottoman Empire was defeated and occupied, its Muslim provinces parceled out among the victorious powers. Persia, though technically neutral, had been overrun by British and Russian forces, sometimes as allies, sometimes as rivals, sometimes as both. The rest of the Muslim world was incorporated in one or other of the great European empires. It seemed that the long struggle between Islam and Christendom, between the Islamic empires and Europe, had ended in a decisive victory for the West.

But the victory was illusory and of brief duration. The West European empires, by the very nature of the culture, the institutions, even the languages that they brought with them and imposed on their colonial subjects, demonstrated the ultimate incompatibility of democracy and empire, and sealed the doom of their own domination. They taught their subjects English, French, and Dutch because they needed clerks in their offices and counting houses. But once these subjects had mastered a Western European language, as did increasing numbers of Muslims in Western-dominated Asia and Africa, they found a new world open to them, full of new and dangerous ideas such as political freedom and national sovereignty and responsible government by the consent of the governed.

These ideas powerfully affected both the subjects and masters of the Western empires, making the one unwilling to accept, the other, to impose, an old-style autocratic domination. In the nineteenth century, these ideas had encouraged the Christian subject peoples of the Ottoman Empire to rebel and demand their independence. In the twentieth century, the same ideas had the same effect on the Muslim subject peoples of the European empires, and this time the imperial masters were forced to recognize their own principles and ideals being used against them.

Some of the movements of revolt against Western rule were inspired by religion and fought in the name of Islam. But the most effective at that time—those that actually won political independence—were led by Westernized intellectuals who fought the West with its own intellectual weapons. Sometimes indeed they fought the West with Western help and encouragement; Western sympathizers played a significant and sometimes forgotten role in the development of Turkish, Arab, Indian, and other nationalisms.

In the areas that they ruled, the British and the French created constitutional and parliamentary regimes in their own image—British-style constitutional monarchies and French-style republics. None of them worked very well, and with independence, almost all of them were discredited and overthrown. In the Russian Empire, revolution and civil war for a while loosened the control of the central government over its imperial territories. But the Soviets succeeded in restoring it with greater authority than ever before, and were much more successful than either the British or the French in establishing Soviet republics in their own image in the Muslim lands that they ruled. Even after the breakup of the Soviet Union, these former Soviet republics have found it more difficult to extricate themselves from the embrace of their former masters, than did the subjects of Britain and France.

During the 1930s, Italy and then, far more, Germany offered new ideological and political models, with the added attraction of being opposed to the Western powers. These won widespread support, and even after their military defeat in World War II, they continued to serve as unavowed models in both ideology and statecraft.

But not for the economy. The victory of the Soviet Union in 1945 suggested a different solution—a return to the economic explanation of Western success, but with a socialist shortcut. State control of the economy was imposed in several countries. Various types of socialism, sometimes called Arab socialism, sometimes called scientific socialism, were adopted. They ended in disastrous failure, in ruination maintained by tyranny. Most people in the region have by now decided that socialism—or at least their experience of it—is neither Arab nor scientific.

Socialism by that name has generally been abandoned, but the high level of state involvement in the economy, which long preceded the adoption of socialism, has long survived its abandonment; it continues to inhibit economic growth. The difference between Middle Eastern and Western economic approaches can be seen even in their distinctive forms of corruption, from which neither society is exempt. In the West, one makes money in the market, and uses it to buy or influence power. In the East, one seizes power, and uses it to make money. Morally there is no difference between the two, but their impact on the economy and on the polity is very different.

The mystery of Western success was still not solved. Could there be something more than modernizing the armed forces, the state that commanded them, and the economy that fed, supplied, and equipped them? In a word, something more than modernity?

conclusion.

3

Social and Cultural Barriers

During the eighteenth and nineteenth centuries and a good part of the twentieth, Middle-Eastern observers, increasingly aware of the disparity in military power between Middle Eastern and Western states, turned their attention primarily to weaponry and the conduct of warfare and then to economic production and government administration, seen as the primary sources of Western preponderance. In looking at these, they tried to find what was most distinctive and different about the Western way of dealing with these matters and thereby to identify the source of Western superiority. In looking for this mysterious source they naturally gave most attention to what was visibly and palpably different from their own way of doing things, and then tried to adopt, adapt, or simply buy it. They began with the visible sources of power and prosperity—military, economic, political. It was in these three areas that they concentrated their main effort—with limited and sometimes indeed negative results.

But there were other differences between Islamic and Western society—greater, more profound, yet somehow for long overlooked or not seen as relevant. I shall try to illustrate three of these aspects by quotations from Middle-Eastern visitors to the West. All three are Turkish, since the Turks were the earliest and for some time the only Muslim travelers in Europe. The first comes from Evliya Çelebi, a famous Turkish writer of his time who visited Vienna in 1665 as part of an Ottoman diplomatic mission. In the course of a long and detailed account of the imperial capital and his adventures there, Evliya describes a "most extraordinary spectacle" that he saw.

In this country I saw an extraordinary spectacle. Whenever the emperor meets a woman in the street, if he is riding, he brings his horse to a standstill and lets her pass. If the Emperor is on foot and meets a woman, he stands in a posture of politeness. The woman greets the emperor, who then takes his hat off his head to show respect for the woman. After the woman has passed, the emperor continues on his way. It is indeed an extraordinary spectacle. In this country and in general in the lands of the unbelievers, women have the main say. They are honored and respected out of love for Mother Mary.[1]

My second example comes from another Ottoman diplomat in Vienna, the ambassador Mustafa Hatti Efendi, who in a report dated 1748 describes a visit to the observatory as guest of the emperor and speaks of some of the "strange devices and wonderful objects" he saw there:

One of the contrivances shown to us was as follows. There were two adjoining rooms. In one there was a wheel, and on that wheel were two large, spherical, crystal balls. To these were attached a hollow cylinder, narrower than a reed, from which a long chain ran into the other room. When the wheel was turned, a fiery wind ran along the chain into the other room, where it surged up from the ground and, if any man touched it, that wind struck his finger and jarred his whole body. What is still more wonderful is that if the man who touched it held another man by the hand, and he another, and so formed a ring of twenty or thirty persons, each of them would feel the same shock in finger and body as the first one. We tried this ourselves. Since they did not give any intelligible reply to our questions, and since the whole thing is merely a plaything, we did not think it worthwhile to seek further information about it.

Another contrivance . . . consisted of small glass bottles which we saw them strike against stone and wood without breaking them. Then they put fragments of flint in the bottles, whereupon these finger-thick bottles, which had withstood the impact of stone, dissolved like flour. When we asked the meaning of this, they said that when glass straight from the fire was cooled in cold water, it became like this. We ascribe this preposterous answer to their Frankish trickery.[2]

My third example comes from an Ottoman ambassador, Vasif Efendi, who was in Spain from 1787 to 1789. Describing his social engagements, he remarks: "During meals . . . [the Spaniards] greatly admired the musicians and singers who accompanied our mission. At the king's command, all the grandees, one after another, invited us to dinner, and we suffered the tedium of their kind of music."[3]

The topics of these three excerpts, women, science, and music, mark three crucial differences in approach, in attitude, and in perception between two neighboring civilizations. Let us look at them more closely.

The difference in the position of women was indeed one of the most striking contrasts between Christian and Muslim practice, and is mentioned by almost all travelers in both directions. Christianity, of all churches and denominations, prohibits polygamy and concubinage. Islam, like most other non-Christian communities, permits both. European visitors to the Islamic lands were intrigued by what they knew or, more accurately, what they heard concerning the harem system, and some of them speak with ill-concealed and ill-informed envy of what they imagine to be the rights and privileges of a Muslim husband and master of the house. Muslim visitors to Europe speak with astonishment, often with horror, of the immodesty and frowardness of Western women, of the incredible freedom and absurd deference accorded to them, and of the lack of manly jealousy of European males confronted with the immorality and promiscuity in which their womenfolk indulge. We find this observation even in the most unlikely places. Thus, for example, a Moroccan ambassador who was in Spain in 1766 speaks of the free and easy ways of Spanish ladies, and the absence of a virile sense of honor among their husbands.[4] If this was his impression of the Court of Spain, one shudders to think of what he would have written had he continued his journey into Europe to, for example, the Court of Versailles.

Evliya Çelebi was expressing a fairly normal Middle-Eastern response to the Austrian Emperor's normal courtesy to a lady, and clearly indicates that he himself would not have believed this improbable story had he not seen it with his own eyes. His explanation of the extraordinary deference given to women in Christendom—that "they are honored and respected out of love for Mother Mary"—should not be dismissed as absurd, especially if one bears in mind that, according to the Islamic tradition, the Trinity, worship of which Islam condemns as near-polytheistic blasphemy, consisted of God, Jesus, and Mary.[5]

Some had even more extraordinary stories to tell. For example Vahid Efendi, who traveled across Europe to Paris as Ottoman ambassador in 1806, describes his journey and the places where he stayed in some detail. Here is one of those details: "At European banquets many women are present. The women sit at table while the men sit behind them, watching like hungry animals as the women eat. If the women take pity on them, they give them something to eat; if not, the men go hungry."[6] I don't know where he heard this story, but it is not more improbable than some of the tales told by Western visitors about what went on in Muslim harems.

The status of women, though probably the most profound single difference between the two civilizations, attracted far less attention than such matters as guns, factories and parliaments. Westerners did not differ greatly from Middle Easterners in this astigmatism.*

According to Islamic law and tradition, there were three groups of people who did not benefit from the general Muslim principle of legal and religious quality—unbelievers, slaves, and women. The woman was obviously in one significant respect the worst-placed of the three.

---

*An interesting example is Verdi's famous opera *Aida*. This opera, it will be recalled, was commissioned by the Khedive Ismail of Egypt and first performed in Cairo on Christmas Eve 1871. The setting was ancient Egypt, about which the composer and his librettist had received guidance from the famous French Egyptologist Auguste Mariette, usually known by his Egyptian title as Mariette Pasha. One of the central problems of the story is the dilemma of the victorious Egyptian general Radamès, torn between the loves of two women—Amneris, the daughter of Pharaoh, and Aida the Ethiopian slave, the daughter of the Ethiopian king with whom Egypt is at war. Caught between these two women, Radamès is driven to treason and finally to death. For a nineteenth century European Christian, this was indeed an agonizing dilemma. It would have been meaningless in Egypt, either in the time of the pharaohs or in Verdi's own day, and the hero could have had both ladies; the princess by marriage as a wife, the slave by gift or purchase as a concubine and perhaps later, as a secondary wife. Were Verdi and his librettist trying to send a subtle message to their Egyptian patrons; or, more probably, were they simply uninformed or unconcerned about the situation of women in Egypt?

Figure 3-1
Turkish lady and Slave in the Harem. From Samuel S. Cox,
Diversions of a Diplomat in Turkey, New York, 1887.

The slave could be freed by his master; the unbeliever could at any time become a believer by his own choice, and thus end his inferiority. Only the woman was doomed forever to remain what she was—or so it seemed at the time.

The rise of Western power and the spread of Western influence brought important changes to all three groups. The Christian powers were naturally concerned with the status of the Christian subjects of Muslim states, and used their great and growing influence to secure for them a status of legal equality and—in fact though not in principle—economic privilege. In this drive for emancipation, Christians were the intended, Jews the incidental beneficiaries.

Slavery was also a concern of the Western powers and most particularly of the United Kingdom, which had abolished slavery in its own empire at the beginning of the nineteenth century and treated slave-trading as an international crime, like piracy, to be suppressed and punished wherever it was met on land or sea. By the late twentieth century, chattel slavery in the Middle East, had, with rare local exceptions, been abolished.

The struggle for women's rights proved much more difficult, and the outcome of that struggle is still far from clear. The European powers, who used their influence and even their armed forces to impose the abolition of slavery and the emancipation of non-Muslims, showed no interest in ending the subjection of women. Nor is there much evidence that either the Middle-Eastern reformers or their European mentors were concerned about this issue. Even the imperial powers, in this as in most other respects, pursued cautiously conservative social policies, and took care to avoid any changes that would mobilize Muslim opinion against them and bring them no advantage. In some areas of intense colonization, such as French North Africa and Soviet Central Asia, a small class of educated Muslims, culturally assimilated to their imperial masters, followed their practice also in the treatment of women. But these were in every sense limited and marginal. In the heartlands of Islam, such progress as was made in women's rights was due entirely to internal forces and to the unaided efforts of Muslim women and men.

Nevertheless the struggle for the emancipation of women made some progress in the socially and economically more advanced parts of the region and has become a major target of different schools of militant Islamic revival. The Ayatollah Khomeini, in particular, gave it a prominent place in his indictment of the misdeeds of the shah and the crimes of his regime. From a traditional point of view, the emancipation of women—specifically, allowing them to reveal their faces, their arms, and their legs, and to mingle socially in the school or the workplace with men—is an incitement to immorality and promiscuity, and a deadly blow to the very heart of Islamic society, the Muslim family and home. The battle continues.

The earliest example that I have been able to find of a principled argument for women's rights occurs in an article by the great nineteenth-century Ottoman writer Namık Kemal, one of the leaders of the Young Ottomans, published in the newspaper *Tasvir-i Efkâr* in 1867:

> Our women are now seen as serving no useful purpose to mankind other than having children; they are considered simply as serving for pleasure, like musical instruments or jewels. But they constitute half and perhaps more than half of our species. Preventing them from contributing to the sustenance and improvement of others by means of their efforts infringes the basic rules of public cooperation to such a degree that our national society is stricken like a human body that is paralyzed on one side. Yet women are not inferior to men in their intellectual and physical capacities. In ancient times women shared in all men's activities, including even war. In the countryside, women still share in the work of agriculture and trade ... The reason why women among us are thus deprived is the perception that they are totally ignorant and know nothing of right and duty, benefit and harm. Many evil consequences result from this position of women, the first being that it leads to a bad upbringing for their children.[7]

Namık Kemal was a young radical when he wrote this article. Very soon after he fled into exile in Paris, where he joined with others in publishing seditious opposition journals. He returned to Turkey in 1870 and embarked on a highly significant career as writer and activist. He did not however return to this particular theme, and devoted most of his energies to the related topics of country and freedom—in other words, of patriotism and liberalism. Namık Kemal and others after him changed, if not their minds, then certainly their priorities.

But not all. In 1899 a remarkable book appeared in Arabic, entitled *The Liberation of Woman*, written by Qāsim Amīn, a young Egyptian lawyer who had studied in Paris and acquired a French girlfriend who seems to have had some influence on him. While there, he became a passionate advocate of women's rights. The theme of his book was the need to raise the condition of women by educating them, and thus giving them access to social life and to the professions. In particular, he proposed to abolish the veil and to reinterpret the Qur'anic provisions that had usually been interpreted as authorizing polygamy, concubinage, and divorce by repudiation. Only by freeing women, he argued, could Muslim society itself be free, since a free society is one in which all its members are free. Despite his attempts to justify these revolutionary propositions in Islamic terms, his book evoked a very strong reaction from the traditionalist establishment in Egypt and elsewhere. But the book continued to be read; it was also translated from Arabic into Turkish and other languages, and had a considerable impact, more especially on the rising generation of women, some of whom were learning to read, and therefore read this book.[8]

The practical changes in the status of women came in various ways and were due to circumstances most of which can be attributed to the ultimate Western example. The abolition of chattel slavery made concubinage illegal, and though it lingered on for some time in remoter areas, it ceased to be either common or accepted. In a few countries, notably Turkey, Tunisia, and Iran under the late shah, even polygamy was in effect outlawed; in many other Muslim states, while still lawful, it has been hemmed in by legal restrictions, and has become socially unacceptable in the urban middle and upper classes, as well as economically impractical for the urban lower classes. Polygamy is now very rare outside the Arabian peninsula, where men have both the means and the opportunity.

The earliest and most extensive progress was in the economic position of women. Even under the traditional dispensation this was relatively good, and certainly far better than that of women in most

Christian countries before the adoption of modern legislation. Muslim women, as wives and as daughters, had very definite property rights, which were recognized and enforced by law.

In recent changes economic needs were a major factor. As Namık Kemal pointed out, peasant women had from time immemorial been part of the workforce; they had in consequence enjoyed certain social freedoms denied to their sisters in the cities. Economic modernization brought a need for female labor; this need was greatly increased during the years of warfare in which the Ottoman Empire was involved between 1911 and 1922, when much of the male population was in the armed forces, and women were needed to carry on the business of life. This also had some consequences for education, and a steady increase in the numbers of women involved as students in colleges and universities. We find, already in the late Ottoman period, women's magazines, written by women for women. Women began in such "women's professions" as nursing and teaching, traditional in Europe and gradually becoming so in the lands of Islam, and in time they began to penetrate into other professions.

But the reaction was growing. Even the enrollment of women in a traditional profession like teaching was too much for some of the militant Islamists. Khomeini, in his sermons and writing both before and after the Islamic Revolution of 1979, spoke with great anger of the inevitable immorality that, he said, would result from women teaching adolescent boys.[9]

Kemal Atatürk, the founder of the Turkish Republic, took exactly the opposite view. In a series of speeches delivered in the early twenties, he argued eloquently for the full emancipation of women in the Turkish state and society. Our most urgent present task, he repeatedly told his people, is to catch up with the modern world. We shall not catch up with the modern world if we only modernize half the population. This was a surprising line of argument in the early twenties, and came from an unlikely source, an Ottoman pasha and general, but also the founder of modern Turkey.

In the Turkish Republic women's rights became part of the official Kemalist ideology and women played an increasing role in public life. Apart from Turkey, the question of political rights was relatively unimportant in a region where, with few exceptions, the precarious parliamentary systems that once existed gave way to more or less autocratic regimes, controlled by either the army or the party. The question of political rights in any case was meaningless in such societies. In Turkey it was not meaningless, and it has remained an important issue.

Westerners tend naturally to assume that the emancipation of women is part of liberalization, and that women will consequently fare better in liberal than in autocratic regimes. Such an assumption would be false, and often the reverse is true. Among Arab countries, the legal emancipation of women went farthest in Iraq and in the former South Yemen, both ruled by notoriously repressive regimes. It has lagged behind in Egypt, one of the more tolerant and open of Arab societies. It is in such societies that public opinion, still mainly male and mainly conservative, has the greatest influence. Women's rights have suffered the most serious reverses in countries where fundamentalists of various types have influence or where, as in Iran and most of Afghanistan, they rule. Indeed, as already noted, the emancipation of women by modernizing rulers was one of the main grievances of the radical fundamentalists, and the reversal of this trend is in the forefront of their agenda.

The emancipation of women, more than any other single issue, is the touchstone of difference between modernization and Westernization. Even the most extreme and most anti-Western fundamentalists nowadays accept the need to modernize and indeed to make the fullest use of modern technology, especially the technologies of warfare and propaganda. This is seen as modernization, and though the methods and even the artifacts come from the West, it is accepted as necessary and even as useful. The emancipation of women is Westernization; both for traditional conservatives and radical fundamentalists it is neither necessary nor useful but noxious, a betrayal of true Islamic values. It must be kept from entering the body of Islam, and where it has already entered, it must be ruthlessly excised.[10]

The difference between modernization and Westernization, particularly but not exclusively in relation to men and women, can be vividly seen in the dress reforms that began at the end of the eighteenth century and have continued, with occasional interruptions, ever

Figure 3-2
Moses Admonishing Korah (cf. Numbers, xvi). From a Persian religious
poem, seventeenth century, Israel Museum, Jerusalem, 79–621.
Moses, representing divine religion, is wearing Persian dress;
Korah, the arrogant and doomed upstart, is in European costume.
Courtesy of the Israel Museum, Jerusalem.

since. The process began when the sultan formed new-style regiments, in Western formations, with Western weapons, commanded by Western-style officers graded in Western-style ranks. It was natural that the sultan should also dress his new army in Western-style uniforms—indeed one of the early documents urging reform explicitly mentions uniforms and their military, especially disciplinary, usefulness, for example, in making it easy to recognize and arrest deserters.

From the military, the clothing reforms spread to the civil service, and bureaucrats were now attired in frock coats and trousers, in place of their previous more comfortable clothing. Only the headgear—the fez, the turban, the kefiya—remained, to symbolize their difference from the West. Anyone who has visited an Ottoman cemetery will recall the headstones, topped with a carved representation of the distinctive headgear of the person buried there, thus identifying the grave of a Janissary officer, a qadi, or other. Headgear remained particularly important in a symbolic, even a religious sense.

But even that has now changed. For a long time, Middle-Eastern soldiers wore European uniforms with Muslim headgear, eschewing Western-style hats and caps with brims and peaks that obstructed Muslim worship and were thus seen as the symbol of the infidel. In those days, *Şapka giymek*, to put on a hat, was the Turkish equivalent of to turn one's coat (i.e. to become a renegade). Now that too has gone. Today, the armed forces, the civil service, and a large part of the urban male population have adopted Western styles of clothing. Even the diplomats of the Islamic Republic of Iran wear Western suits, with only the missing necktie to symbolize their rejection of Western culture and its symbols. For some reason they have given the necktie a symbolic significance, perhaps because of its vaguely cruciform shape.

While the dividing line between Westernization and modernization is sometimes difficult to establish in the attire of men, it is very clear in that of women. Unlike soldiers and civil servants—in the past both exclusively male occupations—women were never compelled to adopt Western dress or to abandon traditional attire. Indeed, if the matter arose at all in public regulations, it was in the form of a prohibition, not a requirement. Nevertheless some women did adopt at least elements of Western dress, and in our own day some items of clothing, notably the headscarf and the veil, have become powerful emotive symbols of cultural choice. They are especially so in Turkey and Iran, the two countries that most clearly formulate the alternative choices and alternative futures that confront the Muslim—and not only the Muslim—Middle East. For men to wear Western clothes, it would seem, is modernization; for women to wear them is Westernization, to be welcomed or punished accordingly.

The Middle-Eastern response to Western science shows interesting similarities with the response to feminism. It also shows striking differences. At first, the one, like the other, was negative, even contemptuous, and Hatti Efendi's comments were not untypical. But the benefits of scientific education, unlike those of female emancipation, were palpable, visible, and immediate, first in military matters, which were the prime concern of the reformers, and then also in other aspects of life. To teach gunnery and seamanship, it was necessary to impart some knowledge of the sciences on which these were based. With the growth and spread of modern military and naval instruction, both teachers and pupils achieved insights and vision beyond those that navigation could afford, with results more penetrating and more explosive than gunfire.

Through the nineteenth century an increasing number of young Muslims, most of them officers or civil servants, most of them Ottoman, began to speak of how Europe, "the smallest of the continents," achieved paramountcy in the modern world through its mastery of the sciences. Some speak more broadly of knowledge—the same word designates both knowledge and science. In an essay published in 1840, Mustafa Sami, a former chief secretary of the Ottoman embassy in Paris, goes a step further and notes with astonishment: "Every European, man and woman, can read and write. All of them, men and women alike, get at least ten years of schooling. There are special schools where even the deaf and dumb are taught to read and write. Thanks to their science, Europeans have found ways of overcoming plague and other illnesses, and have invented many mechanical devices to mass-produce various items."[11] Another Ottoman with diplomatic experience, Sadık Rıfat Pasha, speaks of the importance that

Figure 3-3
Ladies attired for riding
or walking. From E. W. Lane,
Modern Egyptians, vol. i, p. 56.

Figure 3-4
A lady in the dress worn in private.
Lane, p. 52.

Europeans attach to "astronomy, music, medicine . . . and international politics and military knowledge, plants, animals, minerals, and anatomy."[12] He also notes that in Europe one cannot meet anybody who is unable to read and write in his own language. This was probably an exaggeration in mid-nineteenth-century Europe, but a minor one compared with the difference between the conditions he described and the conditions at home.

During the second half of the nineteenth century Ottoman intellectuals placed ever greater emphasis on the importance of science. Some of them went further, and spoke of a conflict between science and what they cautiously called "fanaticism" or even, explicitly, between science and religion. Increasing numbers of European scientific books were translated, often with prefaces insisting on the importance of science for progress.

Materialism and later positivism also found translators and disciples. One popular author was the Anglo-American scientist and philosopher John William Draper (1811–1882) whose history of the conflict between religion and science, published in 1872 in the United States, was published in Istanbul in Turkish translation in 1895. Another much admired European materialist was Friedrich Karl Christian Ludwig Büchner (1824–1899). He and more especially Auguste Comte greatly influenced the political thinking of the Young Turks and their imitators among other Muslim peoples.

And yet, despite all these efforts, and despite the foundation of schools and faculties of sciences in almost all the new universities, the incorporation of modern science—or should one say Western science?—was lamentably slow.

The reluctance of the Islamic Middle East to accept European science is the more remarkable if one considers the immense contribution of the Islamic civilization of the Middle Ages to the rise of modern science. In the development and transmission of the various branches of science, men in the medieval Middle East—some Christian, some Jewish, most of them Muslim—played a vital role. They had inherited the ancient wisdom of Egypt and Babylon. They had translated and preserved much that would have otherwise been lost of the wisdom and science of Persia and Greece. Their enterprise and their openness enabled them to add much that was new from the science and techniques of India and China.

Nor was the role of the medieval Islamic scientist purely one of collection and preservation. In the medieval Middle East, scientists developed an approach rarely used by the ancients—experiment. Through this and other means they brought major advances in virtually all the sciences.

Much of this was transmitted to the medieval West, whence eager students went to study in what were then Muslim centers of learning in Spain and Sicily, while others translated scientific texts from Arabic into Latin, some original, some adapted from ancient Greek works. Modern science owes an immense debt to these transmitters.

And then, approximately from the end of the Middle Ages, there was a dramatic change. In Europe, the scientific movement advanced enormously in the era of the Renaissance, the Discoveries, the technological revolution, and the vast changes, both intellectual and material, that preceded, accompanied, and followed them. In the Muslim world, independent inquiry virtually came to an end, and science was for the most part reduced to the veneration of a corpus of approved knowledge. There were some practical innovations—thus, for example, incubators were invented in Egypt, vaccination against smallpox in Turkey. These were, however, not seen as belonging to the realm of science, but as practical devices, and we know of them primarily from Western travelers.

The changing attitudes of East and West in the development and acceptance of scientific knowledge are dramatically exemplified in the discovery of the circulation of the blood. In Western histories of science, this is normally credited to the English physician William Harvey, whose epoch-making *Essay on the Motion of the Heart and Blood* was published in 1628 and transformed both the theory and practice of medicine. His great discovery was preceded and helped by the work of a Spanish physician and theologian, Miguel Serveto, usually known as Michael Servetus (1511–1553), who owes his place in scientific history to the discovery, published in 1553, of the lesser or pulmonary circulation of the blood. This discovery was anticipated, in surprisingly similar detail, by a thirteenth-century Syrian physician called

Ibn al-Nafīs. Among his writings was a medical treatise in which, in defiance of the revered authority of Galen and Avicenna, he set forth his theory of the circulation of the blood in terms very similar to those later used by Servetus and adopted by Harvey, but unlike theirs, based on abstract reasoning rather than experiment. Modern orientalist scholarship has shown, with a high degree of probability, that Servetus knew of the work of Ibn al-Nafīs, thanks to a Renaissance scholar called Andrea Alpago (died ca. 1520) who spent many years in Syria collecting and translating Arabic medical manuscripts.

Ibn al-Nafīs was a successful and wealthy physician, who died at the age of about 80. A childless widower, he left his luxurious house, his estate, and his library to a Cairo hospital. His book and his theory remained unknown and had no effect on the practice of medicine. Servetus was arrested in Geneva on August 14, 1553, and charged with blasphemy and heresy. The Protestant authorities, and notably Calvin, demanded that he retract his religious opinions or face the consequences. Servetus refused; he was condemned on October 26, 1553, and burned next day as a heretic. His medical work remained, and formed the basis of major scientific advances in the years that followed.[13]

Another example of the widening gap may be seen in the fate of the great observatory built in Galata, in Istanbul, in 1577. This was due to the initiative of Taqī al-Dīn (ca. 1526–1585), a major figure in Muslim scientific history and the author of several books on astronomy, optics, and mechanical clocks. Born in Syria or Egypt (the sources differ), he studied in Cairo, and after a career as jurist and theologian he went to Istanbul, where in 1571 he was appointed *munejjim-bashı*, astronomer (and astrologer) in chief to the Sultan Selim II. A few years later he persuaded the new Sultan Murad III to allow him to build an observatory, comparable in its technical equipment and its specialist personnel with that of his celebrated contemporary, the Danish astronomer Tycho Brahe. But there the comparison ends. Tycho Brahe's observatory and the work accomplished in it opened the way to a vast new development of astronomical science. Taqī al-Dīn's observatory was razed to the ground by a squad of Janissaries, by order of the sultan, on the recommendation of the Chief Mufti.[14]

This observatory had many predecessors in the lands of Islam; it had no successors until the age of modernization.

The relationship between Christendom and Islam in the sciences was now reversed. Those who had been disciples now became teachers; those who had been masters became pupils, often reluctant and resentful pupils. They were willing enough to accept the products of infidel science in warfare and medicine, where they could make the difference between victory and defeat, between life and death. But the underlying philosophy and the sociopolitical context of these scientific achievements proved more difficult to accept or even to recognize.

This rejection is one of the more striking differences between the Middle East and other parts of the non-Western world that have in one way or another endured the impact of Western civilization. At the present time scientists in many Asian countries make important contributions to what is no longer a Western but a worldwide scientific movement. Except for some Westernized enclaves in the Middle East and some scientists of Middle Eastern origin working in the West, the Middle-Eastern contribution—as reflected for example in the internationally recognized journals that are at the cutting edge of scientific progress—compares poorly with that of other non-Western regions or, even more dramatically, with its own past record.

The response to Western music, and the larger question of cultural change that it raises, deserve fuller treatment.[15]

4

Modernization and Social Equality

It is often said that Islam is an egalitarian religion. There is much truth in this assertion. If we compare Islam at the time of its advent with the societies that surrounded it—the stratified feudalism of Iran and the caste system of India to the east, the privileged aristocracies of both Byzantine and Latin Europe to the West—the Islamic dispensation does indeed bring a message of equality. Not only does Islam not endorse such systems of social differentiation; it explicitly and resolutely rejects them. The actions and utterances of the Prophet, the honored precedents of the early rulers of Islam as preserved by tradition, are overwhelmingly against privilege by descent, by birth, by status, by wealth, or even by race, and insist that rank and honor are determined only by piety and merit in Islam.

The realities of conquest and empire, however, inevitably created new elites and in the natural course of events these sought to perpetuate for their descendants the advantages that they had gained. From early until modern times there has been a recurring tendency in Islamic states for aristocracies to emerge. These are differently defined and arise from varying circumstances at different times and in different places. What is significant is that the emergence of elites or castes or aristocracies happens in spite of Islam and not as part of it. Again and again through Islamic history the establishment of privilege was seen and denounced by both severely traditional conservatives and dubiously orthodox radicals as a non-Islamic or even an anti-Islamic innovation.

The egalitarianism of traditional Islam is not however complete. From the beginning Islam recognized certain social inequalities, which are sanctioned and indeed sanctified by holy writ. But even in the three basic inequalities of master and slave, man and woman, believer and unbeliever, the situation in the classical Islamic civilization was in some respects better than elsewhere. The Muslim woman had property rights unparalleled in the modern West until comparatively recent times. Even for the slave, Islamic law recognized human rights—the term "civil rights" has no meaning in the context of those times and places—unknown in classical antiquity, in the Orient, or in the colonial and postcolonial societies of the Americas. But these three basic inequalities remained, established and unchallenged. In the course of the centuries, a whole series of radical movements of social and religious protest arose within the Islamic world, seeking to overthrow the barriers that from time to time arose between highborn and lowborn, rich and poor, Arab and non-Arab, white and black, all regarded as contrary to the true spirit of Islamic brotherhood; none of these movements ever questioned the three sacrosanct distinctions establishing the subordinate status of the slave, the woman, and the unbeliever.

In the Islamic states from early until later times the free male Muslim enjoyed a considerable measure of freedom of opportunity. The Islamic revelation, when it was first carried by the conquerors to countries previously incorporated in the ancient Middle-Eastern empires, had brought immense and revolutionary social changes. Islamic doctrine was strongly opposed to hereditary privileges of all kinds, even including, in principle, the institution of monarchy. And though this pristine egalitarianism was in many ways modified and diluted, it remained strong enough to prevent the emergence of either Brahmans or aristocrats and to preserve a society in which merit and ambition might still hope to find their reward. In later times this egalitarianism was somewhat restricted. The abolition of the Ottoman *devshirme*, the levy of Christian boys to serve in the Janissaries, had closed the main avenue of upward social mobility, while the formation and persistence of such ensconced privileged groups as the urban and rural notables and the ulema restricted the number of openings accessible to newcomers. In spite of this, however, it is probably true that even at the beginning of the nineteenth century a poor man of humble origin had a better chance of attaining to wealth, power, and dignity in the Islamic lands than in any of the states of Christian Europe, including post-Revolutionary France.

There was still opportunity for those who were free, male, and Muslim—but there were severe restrictions on those who lacked any of these three essential qualifications. The slave, the woman, and the unbeliever were subject to strictly enforced legal, as well as social, disabilities, affecting them in almost every aspect of their daily lives. These disabilities were seen as an inherent part of the structure of Islam, buttressed by revelation, by the precept and practice of the Prophet, and by the classical and scriptural history of the Islamic community.

All three—the slave, the woman, and the unbeliever—were seen as performing necessary functions, although there was occasional doubt about the third. Islamic slavery—certainly by the nineteenth century—was often domestic rather than economic, and slaves as well as women thus had their place in family and home life. The rules regulating their status were seen as part of the law of personal status, the inner citadel of the Holy Law.

The position of the non-Muslim, on the other hand, was a public rather than a personal matter, and was differently perceived. The purpose of the restriction was not, as with the slave and the woman, to preserve the sanctity of the Muslim home, but to maintain the supremacy of Islam in the polity and society that the Muslims had created. Any attempt to remove or even to modify the legal subordination of these three groups would thus have challenged the free male Muslim in two sensitive areas—his personal authority in the Muslim home, his communal primacy in the Muslim state.

Slave
Woman
unbeliever
In the course of the nineteenth century, for the first time in Islamic history, voices were raised in favor of all three groups of inferiors, and suggestions were made for the abrogation or at least the alleviation of their status of inferiority. These new trends were due in part to influences and pressures—the two are far from identical—from outside; they were also affected, and in an important sense made possible, by changing attitudes among the Muslims themselves.

The foreign interest in reform was very different for the three categories. The European powers were unanimous in demanding the abolition of the position of legal inferiority assigned to Christians

84

and incidentally also to Jews in the Muslim states, and in using every means at their disposal to persuade Muslim governments to grant equality to all their subjects—meaning of course their free male subjects—without discrimination by religion. Even the czars of Russia, who in the nineteenth century had introduced for their Jewish subjects a levy of male children similar in its recruitment though not in its opportunities to the *devshirme* that the Ottomans had abandoned in the seventeenth century, joined in the chorus. The interest in slaves was far less widespread and was in effect confined to the British, whose interventions were mainly concerned with black slaves from Africa. There is no evidence that any of the powers showed any great interest in improving the status of Muslim women.

The aim of domestic reform and, in the earlier stages, of foreign intervention was not the abolition of slavery, which would have been quite unrealistic, but its alleviation and more specifically the restriction and ultimately the elimination of the slave trade. Islam, in contrast to both ancient Rome and the modern colonial systems, accords the slave a certain legal status and assigns obligations as well as rights to the slaveowner. He is enjoined to treat his slave humanely and can be compelled by a qadi to sell or even manumit his slave if he fails in this duty. The manumission of slaves is recommended as a meritorious act. It is not, however, required, and the institution of slavery is not only recognized but is elaborately regulated by Islamic law. Perhaps for this very reason the position of the slave in Muslim society was incomparably better than in either classical antiquity or nineteenth-century North and South America. Western observers at the time often comment on the relative mildness of Middle-Eastern slavery. A notable example was the Swiss Henri Dunant, the founder of the Red Cross, who visited North Africa in 1860.

But while the life of a slave in Muslim society was no worse, and in many ways rather better, than that of the free poor, the processes by which slaves were acquired and transported often imposed appalling hardships. It was these that drew the main attention of European opponents of the slave trade, and it was to the elimination of this traffic, particularly in Africa, that their main efforts were devoted.

From a traditional Muslim point of view, to abolish slavery would hardly have been possible. To forbid what God permits is almost as great an offense as to permit what God forbids. Slavery was authorized and its regulation formed part of the shari'a; more important, of the central core of social laws, which remained intact and effective even when other sections of the Holy Law, dealing with civil, criminal, and similar matters, were tacitly or even openly modified and replaced by modern codes. It is thus not surprising that the strongest resistance to the proposed changes came from conservative religious quarters and particularly from the holy cities of Mecca and Medina. In their view they were upholding an institution sanctified by scripture and law, and one moreover necessary for the maintenance of the traditional structure of family life.

The reduction and effective abolition of the slave trade in the Ottoman Empire was in the main accomplished in the course of the nineteenth century. The process of emancipation seems to have begun in 1830 when a *ferman* was issued ordering the emancipation of slaves of Christian origin who had kept to their religion. This was, in effect, an amnesty for Greek and other Christian subjects of the Ottoman Empire who had been reduced to slavery as a punishment for participating in the recent risings. Those who had become Muslims were excluded from this emancipation, and remained the property of their owners. Those who were still Christian were set free.[1]

In earlier times, white slaves were brought from Europe, either by purchase or by capture. By the nineteenth century, the great majority of white slaves, however, both Christian and Muslim, came not from the suppression of rebellion but by purchase from the Caucasian lands. Georgians and Circassians were greatly appreciated both in Persia and in the Ottoman lands, the men for battle, the women for pleasure. They arrived either overland or by sea from the Black Sea ports. Their movement and their subsequent fate were beyond the range of interest of the Western powers and were exclusively Ottoman and Persian concerns. This is also true of the Ottoman attempt to deal with this problem, undertaken without external pressure, by force of internal circumstances, and by due process of law. The Ottoman authorities were able to accomplish a substantial improvement in the

Figure 4-1
The Aurat Bazaar, or market, for female slaves in Istanbul.
By Thomas Allom, 1838.

condition of these slaves, amounting ultimately to the effective, though still not legal, abolition of their servile status.[2]

The restriction of the traffic in blacks in contrast seems to have been due very largely to British pressure. A British request in 1846 to Muḥammad Shāh of Persia was rejected on the grounds that Islam permitted slavery and he therefore could not forbid it. Eventually the British and Persian governments reached a compromise agreement, but efforts by the Royal Navy to enforce this agreement in the Persian Gulf and Indian Ocean continued to cause friction. After several limited and local measures, in 1857 the British succeeded in obtaining a major Ottoman *ferman* prohibiting the traffic in black slaves throughout the Empire, with the exception of the Hijaz.[3] The circumstances that led to this exception throw some light on traditionalist attitudes to social equalization.

The movement against slavery in the Islamic lands was due only in part to Western influence. The first Muslim ruler to emancipate the black slaves was the Bey of Tunis, who in January 1846 decreed that a deed of enfranchisement should be given to every black slave who desired it. Among the reasons for this action he notes the uncertainty among Muslim jurists concerning the legal basis for "the state of slavery into which the black races have fallen" and the need to prevent the black slaves "from seeking the protection of foreign authorities."[4] That the first of these was a genuine concern of conscientious Muslims is shown by a striking passage in the nineteenth-century Moroccan historian Aḥmad Khālid al-Nāṣirī (1834–1897), discussing the illegal enslavement of Muslim blacks. Al-Nāṣirī was writing entirely within the context of traditional society but was clearly affected by the new antislavery ideas current at the time. He recognizes the legality of the institution of slavery in Muslim law, but is appalled by its application. He complains in particular of "a manifest and shocking calamity, widespread and established since of old in the lands of the Maghrib—the unlimited enslavement of the blacks and the importation of many droves of them every year, for sale in the town and country markets of the Maghrib, where men traffic in them like beasts, or worse."[5] While conceding that heathens may lawfully be enslaved, al-Nāṣirī reminds his readers that Muslims may not; by now, he argues, a majority or at least a substantial minority of the blacks are Muslims, and since the natural condition of man is freedom, they should be given the benefit of the doubt. The evidence of slave traders is dismissed as interested and unreliable, and the traders themselves are condemned as "men without morals, virtue or religion."

In all those parts of the region that were subject to European rule or dominance, slavery was in time abolished, in practice as well as in law. It remained legal in the Ottoman Empire and in Persia until the early twentieth century; it was finally abolished in Yemen and Saudi Arabia in 1962. Today, in most of the Middle East as elsewhere, chattel slavery is no longer morally and socially acceptable. Even those who demand the restoration of Qur'anic law usually stop short of demanding the application of those particular provisions. There are indeed some places in or near the region where slavery has been restored, but these are peripheral.[6]

The movement for the emancipation of non-Muslims began much earlier, but unlike that for the emancipation of slaves appears initially to have evoked no support in Islamic circles. The process began at the end of the eighteenth century when Bonaparte's expedition and administration in Egypt drew extensively on the services of Coptic and other local Christians. The French seem to have attached little importance to modifying the institution of slavery and many of them indeed bought concubines for their own use, sometimes with unfortunate results.[7] They could not, however, tolerate the continuance of the numerous restrictions and disabilities imposed by Muslim law and tradition on Christians. These were abolished, and through their connections with the French the Christians of Egypt obtained a position considerably better than equality.

This may help to explain the very sharp Muslim reaction against them. Even the contemporary Egyptian historian al-Jabartī, in general an open-minded observer willing to recognize some of the positive aspects of French rule, comments very negatively on the emancipation and employment of Copts in what was tantamount to a termination of the *dhimma*. He was particularly offended by their wearing fine clothes and bearing arms, contrary to old established usage, by their exercising authority over the affairs and even the persons of the Muslims, and generally acting in a way that in his eyes was a reversal of the proper order of things as established by the law of God. While al-Jabartī shows only modified enthusiasm in welcoming the return of Ottoman authority, he rejoices particularly in the restoration of the *dhimma* and of the restrictions it imposed on his Coptic compatriots.[8]

The brief French occupation of Egypt and of some of the Greek islands and, still more, the permanent Russian annexation of Transcaucasia posed entirely new problems for both the Muslims and their *dhimmī* subjects. The appearance of Armenians in the service of the advancing Russian power on the eastern frontier of Turkey, like the employment of Christian and occasionally Jewish subjects of the Ottoman Empire by the Western powers, created new tensions and produced new reasons for Muslim resentment. A similar problem, though on a smaller scale, arose in Persia, where the non-Muslim minorities consisted of Armenians, both Orthodox and Catholic, Nestorians, Zoroastrians, and Jews. They did not however form territorially contiguous majority populations, and therefore did not raise what became a major issue in the Ottoman lands.

The Christian subjects of the Porte now found themselves involved in the pursuit of what were, in the last analysis, mutually exclusive objectives deriving from incompatible philosophies. The status of *dhimmī* or protected non-Muslim subject of the Muslim state was incompatible with the acceptance of the protection or patronage, sometimes even the citizenship, of a foreign power. Both were incompatible with the quest for equality of rights before the law as equal Ottoman citizens. And this in turn was undermined by the parallel trend toward separation, autonomy, or independence in most of the predominantly Christian provinces of the Empire.

Yet despite these and other difficulties, the new idea struck root, and in the course of the nineteenth century the concept of equal citizenship for Ottoman subjects of different religions gradually gained strength. It drew its main support from the continuing and growing pressure of the European powers for reform within the Empire. But it also began to draw by the midcentury on a significant group of reformers among the Muslim Turks themselves, trying to bring their country into line with what they perceived as modern enlightenment.[9] In Persia the movement for "enlightenment" thus interpreted was later and slower, and encountered significant resistance.

The Ottoman Rescript of the Rose Bower, promulgated on November 3, 1839, took a first minor official step in this direction. Dealing with such matters as the security of life, honor and property of the subject, fiscal reform, regular and orderly recruitment into the armed services, judicial reform, and the like, the edict goes on to say that "these imperial concessions are extended to all our subjects, of whatever religion or sect they may be. . . ."[10]

The edict of 1839 was in principle concerned with administering existing laws and enforcing existing rights rather than creating new ones. The notion, however, of the equality of persons of all religions before the law and in the application of the law represented a radical breach with the past and posed some problems of acceptance for Muslims.

The issue became more urgent in a new phase of the reform that began in 1854, and involved significant changes affecting the status of both slaves and unbelievers. To the dismay of many, the Ottoman government indicated its intention to abolish the two major forms of discrimination against non-Muslims—the *jizya*, or poll-tax, which had universally been imposed by Muslim governments on tolerated non-Muslim subjects, and the ban on bearing arms, a restriction of almost equal universality and duration. These reforms were embodied in the new reform charter, the Imperial Rescript issued on February 18, 1856, in which the sultan laid down, in much more explicit terms than previously, the full equality of all Ottomans irrespective of religion, while at the same time reaffirming all the "privileges and immunities accorded in former times by my ancestors to all the Christian communities and other non-Muslim religions established in my empire." It took some time to perceive the inherent contradiction between these two. The resolution of that contradiction came only with the dissolution of the Empire.

These two major reforms, the equalization of non-Muslims and the ban on the traffic in black slaves, came at approximately the same time. By early 1855 the impact of these changes was already affecting the Hijaz, where there was special concern about the measures against slavery. The reduction in the supply of white slaves from the Caucasus, resulting from the Russian conquest, had already caused alarm; this was heightened by the imposition of restrictions on the importation of black slaves from Africa. On April 1, 1855, a group of prominent merchants in Jedda addressed a letter to the leading members of the ulema as well as to the sharīf of Mecca expressing their concern.[11] They referred, with disapproval, to the steps that already had been taken and quoted a rumor that the impending reforms would include a general ban on the slave trade, together with other pernicious and Christian-inspired changes, such as the emancipation of women, permission for unbelievers to live in Arabia, and the toleration of mixed marriages. The ban, along with the whole program of reform of which it was a part, was condemned by the writers of the letter as an offense against Holy Law, the more so since all the black slaves imported from Africa embraced the Muslim religion.

The letter caused some excitement. The sharīf consulted the chief of the Ulema of Mecca, Sheikh Jamāl, and a few months later, when the governor of the Hijaz sent an order to the district governor of Mecca prohibiting the trade in slaves, Sheikh Jamāl issued a *fatwā* denouncing the ban and some other projected or rumored reforms:

> The ban on slaves is contrary to the Holy sharī'a. Furthermore the abandonment of the noble call to prayer in favor of firing a gun, permitting women to walk unveiled, placing divorce in the hands of women, and such like are contrary to the pure Holy Law. . . . With such proposals the Turks have become infidels. Their blood is forfeit and it is lawful to make their children slaves.[12]

The *fatwā* produced the desired effect. A holy war was proclaimed against the Ottomans, and the revolt began. It did not succeed, and by June of the following year it had been completely crushed. The sultan's government had, however, noted the warning, and took steps to forestall a secession of the slave owning Ottoman south.

A letter from the Chief Mufti of Istanbul, 'Ārif Efendi, to "the Qadi, Mufti, Ulema, Sharīfs, Imams and preachers of Mecca" answered the "slanderous rumors":

It has come to our hearing and has been confirmed to us that certain impudent persons lustful for the goods of this world have fabricated strange lies and invented repulsive vanities to the effect that the lofty Ottoman state was perpetrating—almighty God preserve us—such things as the prohibition of the selling of male and female slaves, the prohibition of the call to prayer from minarets , the prohibition of the veiling of women and the concealment of their private parts, the putting of the right to divorce into the hands of women, the seeking of the aid of people who are not of our religion and the taking of enemies as intimates and friends, all of which is nothing but libelous lies. . . .[13]

In the ban on the trade in black slaves promulgated in 1857 the province of the Hijaz was exempted.

The equalization of the non-Muslims, like the restriction of the slave trade, struck at powerful vested interests, not all of them on the Muslim side. For the Muslims it meant the loss of the supremacy that they had long regarded as their right. But for Christians too, or at least for the Christian leadership, it involved the loss of entrenched and recognized privileges. It also involved equalization downward as well as upward, a change not entirely to the taste of some who regarded themselves as standing on the higher rungs of the ladder. A contemporary Ottoman source remarks:

In accordance with this *ferman* Muslim and non-Muslim subjects were to be made equal in all rights. This had a very adverse effect on the Muslims. Previously, one of the four points adopted as basis for peace agreements *(muṣālaḥa)* had been that certain privileges were accorded to Christians on condition that these did not infringe the sovereign authority of the government. Now the question of specific privileges lost its significance; in the whole range of government, the non-Muslims were forthwith to be deemed the equals of the Muslims. Many Muslims began to grumble: 'Today we have lost our sacred national *[milli]* rights, won by the blood of our fathers and forefathers. At a time when the Islamic *millet* is the ruling *millet*, it has been deprived of this sacred right. This is a day of weeping and mourning for the people of Islam.'

As for the non-Muslims, this day, when they left the status of *raya* and gained equality with the ruling *millet*, was a day of rejoicing. But the patriarchs and other religious chiefs were displeased, because their appointments were incorporated in the *ferman*. Another point was that whereas in former times, in the Ottoman state, the communities were ranked, with the Muslims first, then the Greeks, then the Armenians, then the Jews, now all of them were put on the same level. Some Greeks objected to this, saying: 'The government has put us together with the Jews. We were content with the supremacy of Islam.'[14]

It is significant and in no way surprising that the conservatives in the Hijaz, in their sharp reaction against the reforms of the midcentury, lumped actions in favor of the three groups, slaves, women, and unbelievers, together. It is also noteworthy that they are strikingly specific in naming the aspects of female emancipation to which they objected—the right to move around freely, the right to go unveiled, the right to initiate divorce proceedings. No doubt these were the changes mentioned in the rumors reaching their ears.

On the slave and the unbeliever their information was broadly correct, and the changes were as they feared—though not to the extent of admitting non-Muslims to Arabia or permitting mixed marriages between Muslim women and non-Muslim men. Marriages between Muslim men and non-Muslim women were of course permitted by the sharī'a and were not uncommon. On women's rights, however, they seem to have been entirely mistaken. The powers of Europe, so solicitous on behalf of Christians and slaves, remained unmoved by the condition of the female population of the Empire, though it was no doubt known to them, at least in its more picturesque aspects, from an extensive and sometimes prurient literature. The position of women does not seem to figure among the concerns of Western critics of Ottoman and other Muslim institutions. Ottoman liberals and reformers show slightly more concern, but this in the main found literary rather than political or legislative expression. A long time was to pass before the women of the Empire raised their own voices.[15]

In Persia, neither foreign critics nor Muslim liberals and reformers showed much interest in women's rights, but Persian women themselves began the fight for emancipation. A notable figure was Qurrat al-'Ayn[16] (1814–1852), the eldest daughter of an eminent Shi'ite Muslim theologian. She appears to have received a good Islamic education, but became an active follower of the Bāb, the famous Islamic reformer who created what was virtually a new religion in nineteenth-century Persia. Among other offenses, she preached without a veil and denounced polygamy. She was martyred, along with at least 27 other Bābis, and was put to death by torture. A very different figure was the Princess Tāj es-Saltana, the daughter of Nāṣir ed-Dīn Shāh. Educated in the royal household in French as well as in Persian literature, she became keenly aware of the difference in status between the women of the West and the women of Persia. In her writings, principally memoirs and some poems, she denounced the bondage and misery to which her female compatriots were subjected. These seeds fell on fertile soil, and in the events that led to the constitutional revolution in Persia, 1906–1911, women are said to have played an important part. In the words of a contemporary American observer:

> It is not too much to say that without the powerful moral force of these so-called chattels of the Oriental lords of creation, the ill-starred and short-lived revolutionary movement, however well-conducted by the Persian men, would have early paled into a mere disorganized protest. The women did much to keep the spirit of liberty alive. Having themselves suffered from a double form of oppression, political and social, they were the more eager to foment the great Nationalist movement for the adoption of constitutional forms of government and the inculcation of Western political, social, commercial and ethical codes. Equally strange is the fact that this yearning by the people received the support of large numbers of the Islamic priests—a class which stood to lose much of its traditional influence and privilege by the contemplated changes.[17]

In this last respect, the situation has since changed radically.

5

Secularism and the Civil Society

Secularism in the modern political meaning*—the idea that religion and political authority, church and state are different, and can or should be separated—is, in a profound sense, Christian. Its origins may be traced in the teachings of Christ, confirmed by the experience of the first Christians; its later development was shaped and, in a sense, imposed by the subsequent history of Christendom. The persecutions endured by the early church made it clear that a separation between the two was possible; the persecutions inflicted by later churches persuaded many Christians that such a separation was necessary.

The older religions of mankind were all related to—were in a sense a part of—authority, whether of the tribe, the city, or the king. The cult provided a visible symbol of group identity and loyalty; the faith provided sanction for the ruler and his laws. Something of this pre-Christian function of religion survives, or reappears, in Christendom, where from time to time priests exercised temporal power, and kings claimed divine right even over the church. But these were aberrations from Christian norms, seen and reciprocally denounced as such by

---

*The term "secularism" appears to have been first used in English toward the middle of the nineteenth century, with a primarily ideological meaning. As first used, it denoted the doctrine that morality should be based on rational considerations regarding human well-being in this world, to the exclusion of considerations relating to God or the afterlife. Later it was used more generally for the belief that public institutions, especially general education, should be secular not religious. In the twentieth century it has acquired a somewhat wider range of meaning, derived from the older and wider connotations of the term "secular." In particular it is frequently used, along with "separation," as an approximate equivalent of the French term *laicisme*, also used in other languages, but not as yet in English.

royal and clerical spokesmen. The authoritative Christian text on these matters is the famous passage in Matthew 22:21, in which Christ is quoted as saying, "Render therefore unto Caesar the things which are Caesar's; and unto God the things that are God's." Commentators have differed as to the precise meaning and intention of this phrase, but for most of Christian history it has been understood as authorizing the separate coexistence of two authorities, the one charged with matters of religion, the other with what we would nowadays call politics.

In this, the practice of Christianity was in marked contrast with both its precursors and its competitors. In imperial Rome Caesar *was* God, reasserting a doctrine that goes back to the god-kings of remote antiquity. Among the Jews, for whose beliefs Josephus coined the term "theocracy,"[1] God was Caesar. For the Muslims, too, God was the supreme sovereign, and the caliph was his vice-gerent, "his shadow on earth." Only in Christendom did God and Caesar coexist in the state, albeit with considerable development, variety, and sometimes conflict in the relations between them.

The early Christian experience of defying or avoiding authority was not without precedents. The Jews had offered numerous examples of a religion surviving the persecution of a hostile sovereignty—of perseverance as sojourners in the alien land of Egypt, of prophetic protest against their own erring kings, and, in the struggle of the Maccabees, of resistance to foreign—and pagan—conquest and domination. In Persia, Zoroaster initiated a religious and moral change, which in time took over the state. Still further away, in India, the mission of the Buddha and the subsequent work of his missionaries first brought the idea of a universal religion with a message to all mankind. Even pagan Rome offers examples of religiously inspired or religiously expressed opposition to the Roman state, both from independent peoples resisting Roman conquest, and from provincial subjects resisting Roman rule.

None of this is remotely comparable, in extent or in duration, with the long struggle of the early Christians against authority. For three centuries, Christianity was a persecuted religion—different from, sometimes opposed to, and often oppressed by the state authority. In the course of their long struggle, Christians developed a distinctive institution—the church, with its own laws and courts, its own hierarchy and chain of authority. Christians sometimes speak of "The Synagogue" and "The Mosque" to denote the religious institutions of the Jewish and Muslim faiths. But these are inappropriate terms, the projection of Christian notions onto non-Christian religions. For the Jew or the Muslim, the synagogue or the mosque is a building, a place of worship and study, no more. Until modern times and the spread of Christian norms and influence, neither ever had, for its own worshipers, the institutional sense of the Christian term. The same may be said of the temples of other religions.

The conversion of Constantine in the early fourth century and the establishment of Christianity as the state religion initiated a double change; the Christianization of Rome and—some would add—the Romanization of Christ. For the first time, Christians now held authority and had access to the coercive power of the state, which they promptly used to impose the newly formulated Roman orthodoxy on the older churches of the East. But by this time the Christian faith and the Christian church were centuries old, with their character sharply defined and indelibly marked by the experience of the founding generations. The eastern churches had triumphed over pagan persecution. They endured Christian intolerance, and more easily survived the later, milder disabilities imposed on them by Islam.

Throughout Christian history, and in almost all Christian lands, church and state continued to exist side by side as different institutions, each with its own laws and jurisdictions, its own hierarchy and chain of authority. The two may be joined, or, in modern times, separated. Their relationship may be one of cooperation, of confrontation, or of conflict. Sometimes they may be coequal, more often one or the other may prevail in a struggle for the domination of the polity. In the course of the centuries, Christian jurists and theologians devised or adapted pairs of terms to denote this dichotomy of jurisdiction: sacred and profane, spiritual and temporal, religious and secular, ecclesiastical and lay.

Muhammad was, so to speak, his own Constantine. In the religiously conceived polity that he founded and headed in Medina, the Prophet and his successors confronted the realities of the state and, before very long, of a vast and expanding empire. At no time did they create any institution corresponding to, or even remotely resembling, the church in Christendom. But the tension between religious concerns and political needs was often felt, and the resulting polemics and conflicts are a recurring theme in Muslim history.

The first three major civil wars in Islam, as narrated by Muslim chroniclers, appear as a series of unsuccessful attempts to steer the new Islamic state and community in a religiously defined direction. Pious ideals clashed with the needs of government, and soon of empire; religious aspirations were sometimes seen as threatening the stability and continuity of the political society.

The attempts to impose what one might call ecclesiastical constraints on political and military authority failed, causing the retreat of the pietists into either radical opposition or quietist withdrawal, accompanied by a certain disdain for public service. It is for example a topos of Islamic biography of men of religion in the Middle Ages that the pious hero of the narrative was offered an appointment by the ruler and refused it.[2] The offer establishes his reputation, the refusal his piety. Connection with the state was somehow seen as demeaning, and the qadi, appointed by the state, became a figure of ridicule in Islamic folklore.

Less frequently, the attempt was also made the other way, when an Islamic ruler attempted to impose the rule of the state on religion, to choose a particular doctrine and enforce it. The best-known example was the Caliph Ma'mūn (reigned 813–833 C.E.), who tried to create a sort of Erastian Islam. He and his successors failed and the attempt was abandoned. Later, attempts were made by some Ottoman sultans and Persian shahs, but these were rare and atypical.

Such terms as clergy or ecclesiastic cannot properly be applied to Muslim men of religion. These were in time, and in defiance of early tradition and precept, professionalized, and thus became a clergy in a sociological sense. They did not become a clergy in the theological sense. Islam recognizes no ordination, no sacraments, no priestly mediation between the believer and God. The so-called clergyman is perceived as a teacher, a guide, a scholar in theology and law, but not as a priest.

If one may admit, in a limited professional sense, the existence of a clergy, there is no sense at all in which one can speak of a laity among Muslims. The idea that any group of persons, any kind of activities, any part of human life is in any sense outside the scope of religious law and jurisdiction is alien to Muslim thought. There is, for example, no distinction between canon law and civil law, between the law of the church and the law of the state, crucial in Christian history. There is only a single law, the sharī'a, accepted by Muslims as of divine origin and regulating all aspects of human life: civil, commercial, criminal, constitutional, as well as matters more specifically concerned with religion in the limited, Christian sense of that word.

In the upper house of the traditional British parliament sat the lords spiritual and temporal, the former being the bishops. In classical Islam there are no lords spiritual—no bishops, cardinals, popes, no councils, synods, or ecclesiastical courts. Nor do we find in Islamic history political churchmen like Cardinal Richelieu in France, Cardinal Wolsey in England, or Cardinal Alberoni in Spain. For the same reason, there was in classical Islam no hierarchy, though something of the sort has developed in more recent times, under unavowed and no doubt unperceived Christian influence. One may even say that there is no orthodoxy and heresy, if one understands these terms in the Christian sense, as correct or incorrect belief defined as such by duly constituted religious authority. There has never been any such authority in Islam, and consequently no such definition. Where there are differences, they are between the mainstream and the fringes, between orthopraxy and deviation. Even the major division within Islam, between Sunnis and Shī'a, arose over an historical conflict about the political leadership of the community, not over any question of doctrine.[3]

The absence of a native secularism in Islam, and the widespread Muslim rejection of an imported secularism inspired by Christian example, may be attributed to certain profound differences of belief and experience in the two religious cultures.

The first and in many ways the most profound difference, from which all the others follow, can be seen in the contrasting foundation myths—I use this expression without intending any disrespect—of

Islam, Christianity, and Judaism. The children of Israel fled from bondage, and wandered for 40 years in the wilderness before they were permitted to enter the Promised Land. Their leader Moses had only a glimpse, and was not himself permitted to enter. Jesus was humiliated and crucified, and his followers suffered persecution and martyrdom for centuries, before they were finally able to win over the ruler, and to adapt the state, its language, and its institutions to their purpose. Muhammad achieved victory and triumph in his own lifetime. He conquered his promised land, and created his own state, of which he himself was supreme sovereign. As such, he promulgated laws, dispensed justice, levied taxes, raised armies, made war, and made peace. In a word, he ruled, and the story of his decisions and actions as ruler is sanctified in Muslim scripture and amplified in Muslim tradition.

When the Arab Muslims conquered a number of Roman provinces in the Levant and North Africa and Europe, they did not act like the Christianized barbarians from the north, who struggled to preserve something of the Roman state and its laws and made use of the Latin and Greek languages in which their laws and scriptures were written. The Muslims brought their own scripture, in their own language, and created their own state, with their own sovereign institution and their own holy law. Since the state was Islamic, and was indeed created as an instrument of Islam by its founder, there was no need for any separate religious institution. The state was the church and the church was the state, and God was head of both, with the Prophet as his representative on earth. In the words of an ancient and much cited tradition: "Islam, the ruler, and the people are like the tent, the pole, the ropes and the pegs. The tent is Islam, the pole is the ruler, the ropes and pegs are the people. None can thrive without the others."[4]

After Muhammad's death, his spiritual mission was at an end, but his function of leadership, alike in its religious, its political and its military aspects, was assumed by his successors or deputies, the caliphs.[5] In the Muslim perception, there is no human legislative power, and there is only one law for the believers—the Holy Law of God, promulgated by revelation. This law could be amplified and interpreted by tradition and reasoning. It could not be changed, and no

Muslim ruler could, in theory, either add or subtract a single rule. In fact of course they frequently did both, but their action in so doing was always suitably disguised. In time, with the growing complexity of Muslim law and doctrine, and the example of the older religions before them, the Muslims evolved a class of professional men of religion, the so-called *Ulamā*, those who possess *'ilm*, religious knowledge. These were both jurists and theologians, the two being, in essence, branches of the same profession.

At first sight, the classical Islamic order might seem to resemble the so-called Cesaro-Papism of Eastern Orthodox Christendom. The resemblance is more apparent than real. True, the Byzantine *basileus autokrator* or the Russian czar dominated the religious as well as the political establishments. But there was a patriarch, and under the patriarch a hierarchy of metropolitans and bishops and lesser ecclesiastical authorities, each with a delimited territorial and functional jurisdiction. There was no such hierarchy or delimitation of function in classical Islam, and when a semblance of such an order began to appear in the Ottoman Empire, it was clearly a response to the influences of a predominantly Christian environment.

Another relevant difference between Islamic and Christian political notions is the survival, and latterly revival, in the Islamic world, of the religious basis of identity which, in Christian Europe, was to a large extent replaced by the territorial or ethnic nation-state. Nations and countries of course existed in the Islamic world, and there is much evidence, in the literature, of a sense of ethnic, cultural, and occasionally regional identity. But at no time were these seen as forming the basis of statehood or of political identity and allegiance. In the vast and rich historiographic literature of Islam, there are basically three kinds of historical topic. There are universal histories, meaning, with few exceptions, the history of the Islamic *oecumene* and the caliphs and sultans who ruled over it. There are dynastic histories, focused on a ruling family and covering the often extremely variable territories over which it ruled. There are local or regional histories, most commonly of a city and the immediately surrounding district. These last are primarily topographical and biographical. There are no histories however of the Arabs or of Arabia, of the Turks or of

Turkey, of the Iranians or of Iran. These are very ancient entities, but very modern notions. And in the nineteenth and twentieth centuries when, under the impact of new ideas and pressures from abroad, Muslims began to define themselves and their loyalties in national and patriotic terms, it is surely significant that in Arabic, Persian, and Turkish alike, the words used to designate "the nation" are words that had previously been used to designate the religious polity of Islam—and this, despite the available choice of a number of words of primarily ethnic or territorial content.

The reasons why Muslims developed no secularist movement of their own, and reacted sharply against attempts to introduce one from abroad, will thus be clear from the contrasts between Christian and Muslim history and experience. From the beginning, Christians were taught both by precept and practice to distinguish between God and Caesar and between the different duties owed to each of the two. Muslims received no such instruction.

The history of Christianity is much concerned with schism and heresy, and with the conflicts in which the proponents of competing doctrines and the wielders of rival authorities struggled to overcome each other—by persecution when this was feasible, by war when it was not. The story begins almost immediately after the conversion of Constantine, with the christological and jurisdictional conflicts between the churches of Constantinople, Antioch, and Alexandria. It continued with the struggle between Constantinople and Rome, the later struggle between the Papacy and the Protestants, and the further conflicts between different groups of the latter—until, after centuries of bloody strife and persecution, growing numbers of Christians finally concluded that only by depriving the churches of access to the coercive and repressive powers of the state, and by depriving the state of the power to intervene in the affairs of the church, could they achieve any tolerable coexistence between people of differing faiths and creeds.

The Muslim experience was very different. Muslims had of course their religious disagreements, and these on occasion led to strife and repression. But there is nothing remotely comparable with such epoch-making Christian events as the Schism of Photius, the Reformation, the Holy Office of the Inquisition, and the bloody religious wars of the sixteenth and seventeenth centuries, which almost compelled Christians to secularize their states and societies in order to escape from the vicious circle of persecution and conflict. Muslims encountered no such problem, and therefore required no such answer.

The first Muslim encounter with secularism was in the French Revolution,[6] which they saw, not as secular (a word and concept equally meaningless to them at that time), but as de-Christianized, and therefore deserving of some consideration. All previous movements of ideas in Europe had been, to a greater or lesser extent, Christian, at least in their expression, and were accordingly discounted in advance from a Muslim point of view. The French Revolution was the first movement of ideas in Europe that was seen as non-Christian or even anti-Christian, and some Muslims therefore looked to France in the hope of finding, in these ideas, the motors of Western science and progress, freed from Christian encumbrances. These ideas provided the main ideological inspiration of many of the modernizing and reforming movements in the Islamic world in the nineteenth and early twentieth centuries.

From the beginning, there were a few who saw that these ideas could threaten not only Christianity but also Islam, and who gave warning against them. For a long time they had little influence. The minority who were at all aware of European ideas were for the most part profoundly attracted by them. Among the vast majority, the challenge of Western secular ideas was not so much opposed as ignored. It is only in comparatively recent times that Muslim religious thinkers of stature have looked at secularism, understood its threat to what they regard as the highest values of religion, and responded with a decisive rejection.

The strangeness of these ideas to Muslims can be seen in the struggle to find appropriate terms to designate them. The Turks were the first Muslim people to attempt some study of the West and to devise or adapt terms for Western notions and artifacts. The earliest Turkish discussions of secularism use the term *ladini*, literally "non-religious." This is easily confused with irreligious, and Turkish secularists soon realized that the term they had chosen was unnecessarily provocative. They therefore replaced it with a loan word from French—

laique, which in its Turkish form *lâik* remains in use to the present time. The same word is now used in Persian.

But not in Arabic. The Arabs had a rather easier task since Arabic, unlike Turkish and Persian, is a Christian as well as a Muslim language. In several Middle-Eastern countries there are or were sizable Arabic-speaking Christian communities, who produced a substantial Christian-Arabic literature, and devised the necessary Arabic vocabulary to render Christian terms. For a long time, the Christians of the Fertile Crescent wrote the Arabic language in the Syriac script, just as the Jews wrote it in the Hebrew script, and both Judaeo-Arabic and Judaeo-Christian literatures were unknown to the Muslims. Even after the Christians began to use the common Arabic script, their literature for a while remained a largely internal affair. But with the spread of European influence from the nineteenth century, Arabic-speaking Christians, often educated in Western schools and more open to Western ideas, played a key role in their transmission, and the Christian-Arab lexicon provided a significant part of the new vocabulary that went to make up modern Arabic.

One of these Christian terms that passed into common usage was *'ālamānī*, later also *'alamānī*, literally meaning "worldly," from *'ālam*, world. This word served as the equivalent of temporal, secular, and lay alike. A later loan-translation, *rūḥānī*, from *rūḥ*, spirit, served as its counterpart. More recently, its Christian origin and etymology forgotten, *'ālamānī* has been revocalized *'ilmānī*, derived from *'ilm*, science, and misunderstood to denote the doctrine of those who presume to pit human science against divine revelation. It has become a favorite blanket term used by both radical and traditional religious writers, to denote what they see as foreign, neo-pagan, and generally anti-Islamic ideas, imported by Western propagandists and missionaries and their local dupes and agents, to subvert Islamic society and end the rule of the sharī'a. The source of this evil is variously located in Europe or America, in Judaism, Christianity, and communism. The solution is the same for all of these—to remove the alien and pagan laws and customs imposed by foreign imperialists and native reformers, and restore the only true law, the all-embracing law of God. The proponents of this doctrine won power in Iran in 1979. They are, increasingly, a force to be reckoned with in other Muslim countries.

In the secularization of the West, God was twice dethroned and replaced—as the source of sovereignty by the people, as the object of worship by the nation. Both of these ideas were alien to Islam, but in the course of the nineteenth century they became more familiar, and in the twentieth they became dominant among the Westernized intelligentsia who, for a while, ruled many if not most Muslim states. In a nation-state defined by the country over which it ruled or the nation that constituted its population, a secular state was in principle possible. Only one Muslim state, the Turkish Republic, formally adopted secularism as a principle, and enacted the removal of Islam from the constitution and the abrogation of the sharī'a, which ceased to be part of the law of the land. The six former Soviet republics of predominantly Muslim population inherited a rigorously secular system, except in the sense that communism was an established faith. So far most of them show little inclination to Islamize their laws and institutions. One or two other Muslim countries went some of the way toward separation, and several more restricted sharī'a law to marriage, divorce, and inheritance, and adopted modern, mostly West European, laws in other matters.

More recently, there has been a strong reaction against these changes. A whole series of Islamic radical and militant movements, loosely and inaccurately designated as "fundamentalist," share the objective of undoing the secularizing reforms of the last century, abolishing the imported codes of law and the social customs that came with them, and returning to the Holy Law of Islam and an Islamic political order. In three countries, Iran, Afghanistan, and Sudan, these forces have gained power. In several others they exercise growing influence, and a number of governments have begun to reintroduce sharī'a law, whether from conviction or—among the more conservative regimes—as a precaution. Even nationalism and patriotism, which after some initial opposition from pious Muslims had begun to be generally accepted, are now once again questioned and sometimes even denounced as anti-Islamic. In some Arab countries, defenders of what has by now become the old-style secular nationalism accuse the Islamic fundamentalists of dividing the Arab nation and setting Muslim against Christian. The fundamentalists reply that it is the nationalists who are divisive, by setting Turk against Persian against Arab within the larger community of Islam, and that theirs is the greater and more heinous offense.

In the literature of the Muslim radicals and militants the enemy has been variously defined. Sometimes he is the Jew or Zionist, sometimes the Christian or missionary, sometimes the Western imperialist, sometimes—less frequently—the Russian or other communist.[7] But their primary enemies, and the most immediate object of their campaigns and attacks, are the native secularizers—those who have tried to weaken or modify the Islamic basis of the state by introducing secular schools and universities, secular laws and courts, and thus excluding Islam and its professional exponents from the two major areas of education and justice. The arch-enemy for most of them is Kemal Atatürk, the founder of the Turkish Republic and the first great secularizing reformer in the Muslim world. Characters as diverse as King Faruq and Presidents Nasser and Sadat in Egypt, Hafiz al-Asad in Syria and Saddam Hussein in Iraq, the Shah of Persia and the kings and princes of Arabia, were denounced as the most dangerous enemies of Islam, the enemies from within.

The issue was defined with striking clarity in a widely circulated booklet by Muḥammad 'Abd al-Salām Faraj, the ideological guide of the group that murdered President Sadat of Egypt:[8]

> Fighting the near enemy is more important than fighting the distant enemy. In *jihād* the blood of the Muslims must flow until victory is achieved. But the question now arises: is this victory for the benefit of an existing Islamic state, or is it for the benefit of the existing infidel regime? And is it a strengthening of the foundations of this regime which deviates from the law of God? These rulers only exploit the opportunity offered to them by the nationalist ideas of some Muslims, in order to accomplish purposes which are not Islamic, despite their outward appearance of Islam. The struggle of a *jihād* must be under Muslim auspices and under Muslim leadership, and concerning this there is no dispute.
>
> The cause of the existence of imperialism in the lands of Islam lies in these self-same rulers. To begin the struggle against imperialism would be a work that is neither glorious nor useful, but only a waste of time. It is our duty to concentrate on our Islamic cause,

which means first and foremost establishing God's law in our own country, and causing the word of God to prevail. There can be no doubt that the first battlefield of the *jihād* is the extirpation of these infidel leaderships and their replacement by a perfect Islamic order. From this will come release.

At the present time secularism is in a bad way in the Middle East. Of those Middle Eastern states that have written constitutions, only two have no established religion. One is Lebanon, no longer an encouraging example of religious tolerance or secularization. The other, as already noted, is the Turkish Republic, where, while the general principle of separation is maintained, there has been some erosion. The ex-Soviet republics are still struggling with these problems.

Of the remaining Middle-Eastern countries, those that possess written constitutions all give some constitutional status to Islam, ranging from the Islamic Republic of Iran, which gives religion a central position, to the rather minimal reference in the Syrian constitution, which says the laws of the state shall be inspired by the sharī'a. Of the states without written constitutions, principally Israel and the Kingdom of Saudi Arabia, both accord a very considerable place to religion in the definition of identity and of loyalty. If one may briefly compare the two, Saudi Arabia gives a greater place to the application of religious law, Israel allows a far greater political role to the clergy.

I have used the word "clergy." It is of course a Christian word, alien to both the Muslim and Jewish traditions but very much part of present-day Muslim and Jewish realities. This is the result of a long development, the beginnings of which one can see in the Ottoman ecclesiastical hierarchy. In the Ottoman state there was what is sometimes called the religious institution, a hierarchy of religious authorities with territorial jurisdictions, almost equivalent to the see or diocese of a Christian bishop. The appointment of a mufti of a place, with jurisdiction over a territorially defined entity, dates from Ottoman times and almost certainly follows Christian example or responds to Christian influence. Not only were there muftis of places but there was a hierarchy of muftis culminating in the Chief Mufti of Istanbul whom one might reasonably describe as the primate of the Ottoman Empire, the Muslim archbishop of the capital.

Even after the fall of the Ottoman Empire, the practice continued in the Ottoman successor states in the Middle East, where governments appointed functionaries with the title Chief Mufti, exercising religious, one might even say ecclesiastical, jurisdiction over a city, a province, or a country, and playing a political role unknown in classical Islam. One sees it even more dramatically in the ayatollahs of Iran, a title dating from quite modern times and unknown to classical Islamic history. If the rulers of the Islamic Republic but knew it, what they are doing is Christianizing Islam in an institutional sense, though not of course in any religious sense. They have already endowed Iran with the functional equivalents of a pontificate, a college of cardinals, a bench of bishops, and, especially, an inquisition,[9] all previously alien to Islam. They may in time provoke a Reformation.

For more than a thousand years, Islam provided the only universally acceptable set of rules and principles for the regulation of public and social life. Even during the period of maximum European influence, in the countries ruled or dominated by European imperial powers as well as in those that remained independent, Islamic political notions and attitudes remained a profound and pervasive influence. In recent years there have been many signs that these notions and attitudes may be returning, albeit in much modified forms, to their previous dominance.

The term "civil society" has become very popular in recent years, and is used in a number of different—sometimes overlapping, sometimes conflicting—senses. It may therefore be useful to examine Islamic perceptions of civility, according to various definitions of that term.

Perhaps the primary meaning of civil, in the Middle East today, is as the converse of military. This has a special relevance in a place and at a time when the professional officer corps is often both the source and the instrument of power. In this sense, Islamic society, in its inception and in its early formative years, was unequivocally civil. The Prophet and the early caliphs employed no professional soldiers, but relied for military duties on a kind of armed, mostly voluntary militia. It is not until the second century of the Islamic era (eighth century C.E.) that one can speak, with certitude, of a professional army. The caliph, who in early though not in later times occasionally commanded his armies, was nevertheless a civilian. So too was the wazir, who, under the caliph's authority, was in charge of all branches of the government, both civil and military. The wazir's emblem of office was an inkpot, which was carried before him on ceremonial public occasions.

In the later Middle Ages, internal upheavals and external invasions brought changes, which resulted in the militarization of most Islamic regimes. This has persisted to modern times. During the late nineteenth and early twentieth centuries, there was an interlude of civilian, more or less constitutional government, mostly on Western models. During the 1950s and after, these regimes, for the most part, came to an end, and were replaced by authoritarian governments under ultimate military control.

This is however by no means universal. In some countries, as for example Saudi Arabia, traditional monarchies still maintain a traditional civilian order; in others, like Turkey and, later, Egypt, the military themselves prepared the way for a return to civilian government. On the whole, the prospects for civilianization at the present time seem to be reasonably good.

In the more generally accepted interpretation of the term "civil society," civil is opposed, not to religious or to military authority, but to authority as such. In this sense, the civil society is that part of society, between the family and the state, in which the mainsprings of association, initiative, and action are voluntary, determined by opinion or interest or other personal choice, and distinct from—though they may be influenced by—the loyalty owed by birth and the obedience imposed by force. Obvious modern examples are the business corporation, the trade union, the professional association, the learned society, the club or lodge, the sports team and the political party.

Islamic precept, as presented by the jurists and theologians, and Islamic practice, as reflected by the historians, offer a variety of sometimes contradictory precedents. The tradition of private charity is old and deep rooted in Islam, and is given legal expression in the institution of *waqf*. A *waqf* is a pious endowment in mortmain, consisting of some income-producing asset, the proceeds of which are dedicated to a pious purpose—the upkeep of a place of worship, a school, a bathhouse, a soup kitchen, a water fountain, and the like.

The donor might be a ruler or government official; he might equally be, and very often was, a private person. Women, who in Islamic law have the right to own and dispose of property, figure prominently among founders of *waqfs*, sometimes reaching almost half the number. This is perhaps the only area in the traditional Muslim society, in which they approach equality with men. By means of the institution of *waqf*, many services, which in other systems are the principal or sole responsibility of the state, were provided by private initiative. One of the major changes brought by modernizing autocrats in the nineteenth century was to bring the *waqfs* under state control.

In this and other ways modernization in the Middle East has reduced, not increased, the scope for independent and self-supporting associations, and the encroachment of the reinforced modern state has inhibited the development of a real civil society. In the cultural sphere, the state disposes of new and stronger instruments to control the schools, the media, and in general the printed word. This control will no doubt in time be undermined by the electronic media revolution, but for the time being at least it remains effective. In the economy, even after the collapse and abandonment of socialism, state involvement in economic life continues. In most countries in the region, a very large proportion of the population depends, directly or indirectly, on the state for its income. Many of the remainder eke out a precarious and inadequate livelihood from smuggling and other illicit transactions—all part of a extensive black-market economy in which members of the state apparatus may in various ways be gainfully involved.

Islamic law, unlike Roman law and its derivatives, does not recognize corporate legal persons, and there are therefore no Islamic equivalents to such Western corporate entities as the city, the monastery, or the college. Cities were mostly governed by royal officers, while convents and colleges relied on royal or private *waqfs*. There were however other groupings, of considerable vitality and importance in traditional Muslim society. Such, for example are the kin group—family, clan, tribe; the faith group, often linked together by common membership of a sufi fraternity; the craft group, joined in a guild; the ward or neighborhood within a city. Very often these groups overlapped or even coincided, and much of the life of a Muslim city was determined by their interaction.

In the Islamic context, the independence and initiative of the civil society may best be measured not in relation to the state, but in relation to religion, of which, in the Muslim perception, the state itself is a manifestation and an instrument. In this sense, the primary meaning of civil is non-religious, and the civil society is one in which the organizing principle is something other than religion, that being a private affair of the individual. The first European country that actually accorded civil rights to non-Christians was Holland, followed within a short time by England and the English colonies in North America, where extensive, though not as yet equal rights were granted to nonconformist Christians and to Jews. These examples were followed by others, and the libertarian ideas they expressed contributed significantly to the ideologies of both the American and French Revolutions. In time, these ideas were almost universally accepted in Western Christendom. Though few states, other than France and the United States, accepted a formal constitutional separation of religion and the state, most of them observe it in practice.

In the Islamic world, the dethronement of religion as the organizing principle of society was not attempted until much later, and the attempt was due entirely to European influences. It was never really completed, and is perhaps now being reversed. Certainly in Iran, organized religion has returned to something like the status that it enjoyed in the medieval world, both Christian and Islamic.

During the 14 centuries of Islamic history, there have been many changes. In particular, the long association, sometimes in coexistence, more often in confrontation, with Christendom, led to the acceptance, in the later Islamic monarchies in Iran and Turkey and their successor states, of patterns of religious organization that might suggest a probably unconscious imitation of Christian ecclesiastical usage. These Western influences became more powerful and more important after the French Revolution.

The dissemination of French revolutionary ideas in the Islamic world was not left to chance, but was actively promoted by successive French regimes, both by force of arms, and, much more effectively, by translation and publication. The penetration of Western ideas into the Islamic world was greatly accelerated when, from the early nineteenth century, Muslim students in increasing numbers were sent to institutions of higher education in France, Italy, and Britain, and later also in other countries. Many of these, on their return home, became carriers of infectious new ideas.

Until the impact of these ideas, the notion of a non-religious society as something desirable or even permissible was totally alien to Islam. Other religious dispensations, namely Christianity and Judaism, were tolerable because they were earlier and superseded versions of God's revelation, of which Islam itself was the final and perfect version, and therefore lived by a form—albeit incomplete and perhaps debased—of God's law. Those who lacked even this measure of religious guidance were pagans and idolaters, and their society or polity was evil. Any Muslim who sought to join them or imitate them was an apostate.

One of the tests of civility is surely tolerance—a willingness to coexist with those who hold and practice other beliefs. John Locke, and most other Westerners, believed that the best way to ensure this was to sever or at least to weaken the bonds between religion and the state power. In the past, Muslims never professed any such belief. They did however see a certain form of tolerance as an obligation of the dominant Islamic religion. "There is no compulsion in religion" runs a much quoted verse in the Qur'an (2:256), and this was generally interpreted by Muslim jurists and rulers to authorize a limited measure of tolerance for certain specified other religious beliefs, without of course in any way questioning or compromising the primacy of Islam and the supremacy of the Muslims.

Does this mean that the classical Islamic state was a theocracy? In the sense that Britain today is a monarchy, the answer is certainly yes. That is to say, that, in the Muslim conception, God is the true sovereign of the community, the ultimate source of authority, the sole source of legislation. In the first extant Muslim account of the British House of Commons, written by a visitor who went to England at the end of the eighteenth century, the writer expresses his astonishment at the fate of a people who, unlike the Muslims, did not have a divine revealed law, and were therefore reduced to the pitiable expedient of enacting their own laws.[10] But in the sense of a state ruled by the church or by priests, Islam was not and indeed could not be a theocracy. In this sense, classical Islam had no priesthood, no prelates who might rule or even decisively influence those who did. The caliph, who was head of a governing institution that was state and church in one, was himself neither a jurist nor a theologian, but a practitioner of the arts of politics and sometimes of war. The office of ayatollah is a creation of the nineteenth century; the rule of Khomeini and of his successor as "supreme jurist" an innovation of the twentieth.

In most tests of tolerance, Islam, both in theory and in practice, compares unfavorably with the Western democracies as they have developed during the last two or three centuries, but very favorably with most other Christian and post-Christian societies and regimes. There is nothing in Islamic history to compare with the emancipation, acceptance, and integration of other-believers and non-believers in the West; but equally, there is nothing in Islamic history to compare with the Spanish expulsion of Jews and Muslims, the Inquisition, the *Auto da fé's*, the wars of religion, not to speak of more recent crimes of commission and acquiescence. There were occasional persecutions, but they were rare, and usually of brief duration, related to local and specific circumstances. Within certain limits and subject to certain restrictions, Islamic governments were willing to tolerate the practice, though not the dissemination, of other revealed, monotheistic religions. They were able to pass an even severer test, by tolerating divergent forms of their own. Even polytheists, though condemned by the strict letter of the law to a choice between conversion and enslavement, were in fact tolerated, as Islamic rule spread to most of India. Only the total unbeliever—the agnostic or atheist—was beyond the pale of tolerance, and even this exclusion was usually only enforced when the offence became public and scandalous. The same standard was applied in the tolerance of deviant forms of Islam.

In modern times, Islamic tolerance has been somewhat diminished. After the second Turkish siege of Vienna in 1683, Islam was a retreating, not an advancing force in the world, and Muslims began to feel threatened by the rise and expansion of the great Christian empires of Eastern and Western Europe. The old easy-going tolerance, resting on an assumption not only of superior religion but also of superior power, was becoming difficult to maintain. The threat that Christendom now seemed to be offering to Islam was no longer merely military and political; it was beginning to shake the very structure of Muslim society. Western rulers, and, to a far greater extent, their enthusiastic Muslim disciples and imitators, brought in a whole series of reforms, almost all of them of Western origin or inspiration, which increasingly affected the way Muslims lived in their countries, their cities and villages, and finally in their own homes.

These changes were rightly seen as being of Western origin or inspiration; the non-Muslim minorities, mostly Christian but also Jewish, were often seen, sometimes also rightly—as agents or instruments of these changes. The old pluralistic order, multidenominational and polyethnic, was breaking down, and the tacit social contract on which it was based was violated on both sides. The Christian minorities, inspired by Western ideas of self-determination, were no longer prepared to accept the tolerated but inferior status accorded to them by the old order, and made new demands—sometimes for equal rights within the nation, sometimes for separate nationhood, sometimes for both at the same time. Muslim majorities, feeling mortally threatened, became unwilling to accord even the traditional measure of tolerance. By a sad paradox, in some of the semi-secularized nation-states of modern times, the non-Muslim minorities, while enjoying complete equality on paper, in fact have fewer opportunities and face greater dangers than under the old Islamic yet pluralistic order. The present regime in Iran, with its ruling clerics, its executions for blasphemy, its consecrated assassins, represents a new departure in Islamic history. In the present mood, a triumph of militant Islam would be unlikely to bring a return to traditional Islamic tolerance—and even that would no longer be acceptable to minority elements schooled on modern ideas of human, civil, and political rights. The emergence of some form of civil society would therefore seem to offer the best hope for decent coexistence based on mutual respect.

Secularism in the Christian world was an attempt to resolve the long and destructive struggle of church and state. Separation, adopted in the American and French Revolutions and elsewhere after that, was designed to prevent two things: the use of religion by the state to reinforce and extend its authority; and the use of the state power by the clergy to impose their doctrines and rules on others. This is a problem long seen as purely Christian, not relevant to Muslims or for that matter to Jews, for whom a similar problem has arisen in Israel. Looking at the contemporary Middle East, both Muslim and Jewish, one must ask whether this is still true—or whether Muslims and Jews may perhaps have caught a Christian disease and might therefore consider a Christian remedy.

6

Time, Space, and Modernity

In a letter written in 1554, Ogier Ghiselin de Busbecq, ambassador from the Emperor to the Sultan, describes a problem he encountered on his journey to the Ottoman capital:

> There remained one annoyance, which was almost worse than a lack of wine, namely, that our sleep used to be interrupted in a most distressing manner. We often had to rise early, sometimes even before it was light, in order to arrive in good time at more convenient halting-places. The result was that our Turkish guides were sometimes deceived by the brightness of the moon and waked us with a loud clamour soon after midnight; for the Turks have no hours to mark the time, just as they have no milestones to mark distances. They have, it is true, a class of men called *talismans*, attached to the service of their mosques, who make use of water-clocks. When they judge from these that dawn is at hand, they raise a shout from a high tower erected for the purpose, in order to exhort and invite men to say their prayers. They repeat the performance half-way between sunrise and midday, again at midday, and half-way between midday and sunset, and finally at sunset, uttering, in a tremulous voice, shrill but not unpleasing cries, which are audible at a greater distance than one would imagine possible. Thus the Turkish day is divided into four periods, which are longer or shorter, according to the time of year; but at night there is nothing to mark the time. Our guides, as I have said, misled by the brightness of the moon, would give the signal for packing-up long before sunrise. We would then hastily get up, so that we might not be late or be blamed for any untoward incident that might occur; our baggage would be collected, my bed and the tents hurled into the carriage, our horses harnessed, and we ourselves girt up and ready awaiting the signal for departure. Meanwhile the Turks, having

realized their mistake, had returned to their beds and their slumbers. . . . I dealt with this annoyance by forbidding the Turks to disturb me in future, and undertaking to wake the party at the proper time, if they would warn me overnight of the hour at which we must start. I explained to them that I had clocks which never failed me, and would arrange matters, taking the responsibility of letting them sleep on; they could, I said, safely trust me to get up. They assented, but were still not quite at their ease; they arrived in the early morning, and, waking my valet, begged him to go and ask me 'what the fingers of my timepiece said'. He did this, and then indicated as best he could whether a long or a short time remained before the sun would rise. When they had tested us once or twice and found that they were not deceived, they relied on us henceforward and expressed their admiration of the trustworthiness of our clocks. Thus we could enjoy our sleep undisturbed by their clamour.[1]

In a later letter, written in 1560, Busbecq noted: ". . . no nation has shown less reluctance to adopt the useful inventions of others; for example, they have appropriated to their own use large and small cannons and many other of our discoveries. They have, however, never been able to bring themselves to print books and set up public clocks. They hold that their scriptures, that is, their sacred books, would no longer be scriptures if they were printed; and if they established public clocks, they think that the authority of their muezzins and their ancient rites would suffer diminution."[2]

Another European traveller, Jean Chardin, who visited Persia in 1674, is quoted in 1683 by the English diarist John Evelyn as saying that the Persians "had neither clocks nor watches."[3]

Busbecq's characterization of Turkish, and more generally, of the Middle-Eastern attitudes to the measurement of time and space was no doubt exaggerated, but not entirely false. A characteristic noticed by many travellers was the extreme variability of the weights and measures in common use. The English Arabist Edward William Lane, who spent a good deal of time in Egypt between 1833 and 1835 and wrote extensively on the country and its people, noted: "Of the measures and weights used in Egypt I am not able to give an exact account; for, after diligent search, I have not succeeded in finding any two specimens of the same denomination perfectly agreeing with each other, and generally the difference has been very considerable."[4]

There was indeed wide variation. The *raṭl*, the commonest measure of weight in the marketplace, roughly the equivalent of the European pound, could differ considerably according to the commodity that was being weighed and the place where this was done. The same applied to measures of capacity. To confuse matters further, the same names were used with different values. Similar difficulties arise in dealing with the linear measurements used to indicate length and distance.

Medieval Islam inherited a considerable body of scientific knowledge from classical antiquity and, more remotely, from the ancient civilizations of the Middle East. To this they added new knowledge achieved by their own experiments and researches, notably in cartography, geography, geometry, and astronomy. The last-named in particular involved delicate and precise calculations of both time and space. But all this seems to have had little effect on the everyday calculation of time and distance for practical purposes, for which simpler and more basic methods were used.

Linear measurements were basically of three categories. The first, on a small scale, was commercial and practical in purpose, for measuring cloth and similar commodities, and in building. It was normally expressed in terms of parts of the human body: the finger, the fist, the span, the cubit or ell, the forearm, the fathom (i.e., the distance from fingertip to fingertip of outstretched arms).

A second use of linear measurement, requiring somewhat larger units, was to define enclosed areas. Such measures were required for cadastral and fiscal purposes, and to delimit land held in freehold or, more commonly, under some kind of grant. For the collection of taxes and the allocation of responsibility, somewhat more precise measures were needed than for either trade or travel. Measures in use in earlier times were based mainly on agriculture—some on the amount of land that could be sown with a given quantity of seed, others, more commonly, on the area that could be plowed in a given period of time.

The same use of time spent to indicate distance covered dominates the discussion of what one might call geographic distance. Geographers and cartographers had their systems, mostly derived from classical antiquity, but these were too arcane and too uncertain for most practical purposes. In the literature of travel, in the histories, in public and private correspondence, distance between places is almost invariably measured in terms of time, the basic units being the hour and the day. But days vary in length according to season; the hour, an arbitrary, man-made division, has different meanings; and the distance travelled in even a fixed hour or day will be affected—indeed determined—by the terrain and the traveler.

Measures of distance for travel drew on the human body in movement; thus the old Persian *farsakh*, which appears in Greek as *parasang*, was defined as the distance a man could cover on foot in an hour, while the Arabic *marḥala* (Turkish *konak*) was the distance a traveler could cover in a day. In the former Byzantine provinces the Muslim government for a while retained the Roman mile, in Arabic called *mīl*. In these too there was an attempt to establish relationships—the *farsakh* was said to be three miles, the mile a hundred fathoms.

The habit of measuring distances in time and motion has survived to the present day. It is not unusual, if one asks a peasant how far it is to the next village, to be told "one cigarette"—meaning that if you light a cigarette now, by the time you finish it you will be in the village.

Busbecq was mistaken in thinking that there were no milestones. The earliest Islamic milestones are dated 86 A.H. (705 C.E.) and were erected by the caliph 'Abd al-Malik in the district of Jerusalem. Two of them point to Jerusalem, one at seven miles, the other at eight miles from the city. The other two point to Damascus, at 107 and 109 miles.[5] These represent a relic of the past, and the use of miles and of milestones had in general little impact in the Islamic Middle East. The word "mile," Arabic *mīl*, remained in use but was, so to speak assimilated. Arabic lexicographers define it as the distance to which the eye can reach along land. Some assess this at 3,000 cubits, others at 4,000 cubits. Using different cubits, they agree that its extent is 96,000 fingers. Even if Busbecq was technically in error, his exasperation is understandable.

The situation regarding the measurement of time is not much better. The day, the month, and the year are of course fixed by nature, though it may be noted in passing that for Muslims as for Jews, the day begins at sunset: "and the evening and the morning were the first day" (Genesis 1:5). For measuring anything less than a day or more than a year, human ingenuity provided answers—at one end the clock to divide the day, at the other the calendar to count the years. The subdivisions of the day are thus conventional, and considerable differences arise.

The principal subdivision of the day, the hour (Arab *sā'a*, Aramaic *sha'ta*, Hebrew *sha'a*) was already known in antiquity. In the Hebrew Bible the word only occurs five times, all of them in the Book of Daniel—that is to say, after the Babylonian captivity, when the Jews came under the influence of Babylonian culture. Of the five, four (Chapter 3:6;15; 4:30; 5:5) all refer to something happening at the same moment as something else. Only in one occurrence (Daniel 4:16) does the word appear to indicate a unit of time.

In Talmudic literature, the word is already extensively used to mean one of a sequence of numbered subdivisions of the day or of the night—but how many, and of what length, is not always clear.

In the Qur'ān, the word *sā'a* occurs no less than 47 times, 33 of them referring to the "last hour" and therefore retaining the earlier meaning of a moment or instant.

At some unspecified but almost certainly early date, the Arabs adopted the notion that the day was divided into 24 hours. These hours were of two kinds: temporal, i.e., varying according to the season, or fixed and equal. In a civilization comparatively close to the equator, the temporal discrepancies were less important than in the remoter lands of Europe. By Ottoman times a compromise was in use, whereby the day was divided into 24 equal hours, but the reckoning, in accordance with old tradition, started at sunset. This meant that in principle clocks had to be reset every day. This arrangement is sometimes referred to by travellers as "Turkish time" or "Arab time." The two systems of reckoning time remained in use to the present day, but the increasingly general adoption of clocks and watches is gradually eliminating the variable clock.

Apart from the natural, usually observable, demarcation of the day by dawn, noon, and sunset, one other subdivision was of crucial importance for Muslims, and that was the fixing of the times of prayer.

In the same way, one of the most basic purposes of the geographical sciences was to determine the direction of prayer, i.e., of Mecca. This was especially important in newly Islamized countries, where there was no established tradition.

The five daily prayers toward Mecca are one of the basic religious obligations of every Muslim. Communal prayer takes place once a week, on Friday. On the other days the individual prays, if necessary alone, wherever he may be. The time is stated as a band rather than a moment, and is determined by observation. The times of the five prayers are 1: the predawn prayer, before the sun appears; 2: the noon prayer, when the sun passes the zenith; 3: the afternoon prayer, when the shadows cast by objects are equal to their height; 4: the sunset prayer, after the sun has disappeared beneath the horizon, and 5: the evening or night prayer, after the disappearance of the last light. The exact observation of these phenomena is therefore of paramount importance, and will obviously be much affected by regional and seasonal differences. From early times, Muslim scholars and scientists devoted considerable efforts to determining and tabulating the correct times and direction of prayer. At one level, this was done by simple observation; at another by the devising of instruments and the preparation of tables.

Apart from prayer, there were few other activities that required even approximate timing. This was a society in which there were no parliaments, councils, or municipalities, and the conduct of public business required no kind of schedule. The nearest approach to a council, the Ottoman Imperial Divan, met four days a week, on Saturday, Sunday, Monday, and Tuesday. According to contemporary descriptions, it began its proceedings at daybreak and continued until about noon, when the petitioners and other outsiders withdrew, and lunch was served to the members of the Divan, who then went on to discuss what business remained. In schools and colleges, the teaching day was of course punctuated and regulated by the prayers. Travel, for caravans or for individuals, was again structured around the prayers and, ultimately, the three points of the day—sunrise, noon, and sunset.

An important figure at the courts of some Middle-Eastern rulers was the *Munajjim*, who combined the functions of astrologer and astronomer. In the first capacity he was concerned with fixing astrological times—that is to say, he had to choose auspicious times for starting a new venture—a wedding, a military campaign, a journey, and the like. In his capacity as astronomer, he was responsible for keeping and, where necessary, correcting the astronomical tables and establishing some sort of relationship between astronomical and practical time.

The use of devices to measure the passage of time was by no means new in the Middle East. The ancient Greeks used two devices for measuring time, the sundial and the water clock. Both of them were invented in the Middle East—the sundial, according to Herodotus, by the Babylonians, the water clock by the Egyptians. The sundial tells the time by the changing length and direction of the shadow and varies therefore according to the season and the place. Greek mathematicians devised several ways of coping with these two problems. The sundial was of course useless between sunset and sunrise, or when the sun was hidden, and there was no remedy for that. The water clock—a place or a device where water leaks at a regular pace—had the advantage that it also worked in the dark, but it posed problems of care and maintenance. Here, too, the Greek mathematicians devoted considerable ingenuity in inventing automata to tell the time by water, some of them with musical accompaniment. Medieval Muslim scientists added some new, rather elaborate, devices of their own. Some of these even found their way to Europe, where they were treasured more as works of art than as objects for everyday use.

The mechanical clock was a product of Europe, where it was first attested at the beginning of the fourteenth century. The spread of European clocks to the Middle East was a slow process. The Ottoman Sultan Mehmed II is alleged to have shown some interest; the same is said of Sultan Süleyman the Magnificent, to whom, in 1547, the French king sent a "great clock made in Lyons where there was a fountain which in the space of twelve hours drew the water that had been put there, and was a masterpiece of high price."[6]

By the sixteenth century, European clocks and watches were widely used in the Middle East. They were found particularly useful in mosques, to fix the times of the five daily prayers. Taqī al-Dīn, the creator of the Istanbul observatory, even wrote a treatise on clocks operated by weights and springs. In the mid- and late- seventeenth centuries there was a guild of clockmakers and watchmakers in Istanbul. They were however emigrés from Europe, not local, and by the end of the seventeenth century they were no longer able to compete with imports from Europe, where manufacturers were designing special clocks and watches for the Middle-Eastern market, and were steadily improving the quality of pendulum clocks and spring-driven watches, with which local clockmakers could not compete. Voltaire, in his correspondence, has some interesting references to watchmakers living on his estate at Ferney, who with his help exported their products to Turkey.

During the seventeenth and eighteenth centuries clocks figure with increasing frequency, first among the gifts presented by European embassies and companies to Middle-Eastern monarchs and notables, and then as articles of commerce. Maintenance and repair of these unfamiliar devices were of course a problem, and all too often, when clocks for one reason or another ceased to function, they were neglected and abandoned. The practice arose of sending craftsmen along with the gift of clocks, to demonstrate their use and to repair them when necessary. Some even established residence in Turkey and, to a much lesser extent, in Persia. In some of the commercial agreements and treaties between European and Middle-Eastern governments, the European parties undertook to send clockmakers and watchmakers as well as clocks and watches.

In the eighteenth century, if not earlier, there were many clocks and watches in private possession, as is attested by the inventories of the estates of deceased persons. A tabulation of Western-made articles in these inventories in Istanbul puts clocks and watches in first place, almost double the number of pistols and muskets, which come second. Binoculars, telescopes, and eyeglasses come later in the list, in much smaller quantities.[7]

By the nineteenth century European clocks and watches were in general use—but all were in government or private possession. The practice of establishing public clocks in towers or other structures remained alien. A few are reported in some of the Balkan provinces of the Ottoman Empire, where most of the inhabitants were Christian—some of them indeed dating from before the Ottoman conquest. But these were local and without impact elsewhere.

A public clock, set up in the market of Isfahan, constructed by an Englishman by order of Shāh ʿAbbās (1587–1629) was apparently of brief duration. It was not until the middle of the nineteenth century that the first public clock in Istanbul—perhaps indeed in any Islamic country—was installed in the grounds of the Dolmabahçe Palace. And at about the same time, in 1854, a clock tower was built in the citadel of Cairo equipped with a clock received some time earlier, as a gift from the French King Louis Philippe to the Egyptian ruler Muḥammad ʿAlī Pasha.

As always with a borrowed technology and its culture, there was a time lag in the measurement of time. This problem was aggravated by the general change in the Islamic world. Some centuries earlier, the Islamic Middle East had led the world in science and technology, including devices for measuring time. But Middle-Eastern technology and science ceased to develop, precisely at the moment when Europe and more specifically Western Europe was advancing to new heights.

The disparity was gradual, but progressive. By the late eighteenth century, watchmakers in Istanbul were able to produce clocks and watches of the type made in Europe in the early seventeenth century. In this as in much else they were unable to keep pace with the rapidly advancing West.

The week, like the hour, is unrelated to natural phenomena. For Jews, Christians, and Muslims, it is defined by scripture, and its concluding day of rest and/or public prayer is differently determined—Saturday for Jews, Sunday for Christians, Fridays for Muslims. Even the measurement of the passing of months and years still leaves some scope for religious regulation and human ingenuity. Already in antiquity, astronomers noted the discrepancy between the lunar and solar years, and devised a number of ways of bridging it, of which the best known is the leap year. For religious purposes, Islam, unlike Judaism and Christianity, established a purely lunar calendar, with the result that all the Islamic festivals rotate through the entire solar year three times a century. This calendar is reckoned from the beginning of the

Arabian year in which the *Hijra*, the migration of the Prophet from Mecca to Medina, took place.

Being purely lunar, the *Hijra* calendar caused some practical difficulties in public administration, particularly at a time when taxation depended mainly on agriculture, which in turn is determined by the rotation of the seasons. Muslim governments therefore, from early times, adopted a number of different solar calendars, which were used for administrative purposes, alongside the religious lunar calendar. Some were pre-Islamic, such as the solar calendars in use at the time of the conquest in Egypt and Iran. Others were post-Islamic. The Ottoman *maliye* or financial year was a solar adaptation of the Muslim era, using Muslim dates with Eastern Christian months. Dating from 1790 C.E., it remained in use almost until the end of the Empire. A Persian compromise, combining the Muslim year with old Persian months, remains in use in Iran to the present day. In both of these, discrepancies inevitably arose between the true Muslim lunar reckoning and the adapted solar Muslim year. Thus, for example, the Young Turk revolution of 1908 occurred in 1326 of the *Hijra* and 1324 of the *maliye* era; the Iranian revolution of 1979, in 1399 of the *Hijra*, and 1358 of the Iranian solar calendar.

Private and business correspondence, as far as one can ascertain, were dated according to the Muslim calendar, but fiscal records were kept according to one or more solar calendars. Until the nineteenth century, diplomatic documents carried Muslim lunar dates—but these sometimes show a curious imprecision. Ottoman royal letters and other missives indicate the year by number and the month by name. The day however is normally indicated as the first of the month, the last of the month, or the first, middle, or last decade of the month.

With such difficulties and their equivalents elsewhere, it is hardly surprising that the Christian calendar, in its Gregorian version, is now generally accepted for almost all public and governmental functions—by Muslims and Jews in the Middle East, and by non-Christians everywhere else in the world. The universalization of this era is symbolized by the replacement of A.D. and B.C. by C.E. (Common Era) and B.C.E. in international usage.

As well as time, Western influence also affected the measurement, perception, and use of space. This difference can be seen immediately in the contrast between European and Islamic art, notably in the artist's perception and use of perspective. In this respect, European influence can be discerned at an early date in Turkish and Persian painting, both miniature and mural.

The perception of space was much affected by the introduction of two European devices for improving vision—reading glasses and telescopes. The first are attested as early as the fifteenth century and as far east as Iran, where the poet Jāmī, lamenting the infirmities of old age, remarks that his eyes were now useless "unless, with the aid of Frankish glasses, the two become four."[8] Middle-Eastern soldiers and officials were quick to appreciate the value of telescopes for military purposes and later, in combination with other devices, for demarcation. This made it possible to introduce what was previously a purely European idea—that of a precisely demarcated frontier.

Medieval states did not have frontiers in the modern sense. On land as in time, there was no precise line of demarcation, but rather a zone, a band, or interval. This was sufficient for all practical purposes. Islamic laws regulating relations within and between states deal with people, not places. A ruler ruled as far as he could collect taxes and maintain order. Where there were no taxes to collect, the precise boundary didn't matter. Deserts were regarded in much the same way as the sea. The notion of a frontier and the possibility of precise demarcation came from Europe, along with the idea that such demarcation was both possible and necessary. The Ottoman and Persian Empires were in a state of intermittent conflict for some 400 years, but it was not until 1914 that, with the help of a joint Anglo-Russian commission of experts, they finally demarcated a frontier between them. That frontier still marks the western borders of Iran, with Turkey in the north and with Iraq in the south, where it gave rise to some frontier disputes.

Western perceptions—and measurement—of time and space also had an impact on art and music. We can see the influences of European art on the miniature at quite an early date, even as far east as Iran. One of the attractions of Western art and particularly of Western portraiture must surely have been the use of perspective, which made possible a degree of realism and accuracy unattainable in the stylized and rather formal art of the traditional miniature. Pictures of the Ka'ba in Mecca, the holiest shrine of Islam, were widely disseminated in the Ottoman lands and elsewhere. These were of course schematic representations. Sometime in the early eighteenth century a European artist, presumably having obtained one of these pictures, redrew it in the European style, that is, in perspective. It appears on a musical clock, made in England for the Turkish market.[9]

In the late eighteenth and early nineteenth century, Western influence becomes very clear, both in the structure of buildings and in their interior decoration. By the nineteenth century it is almost universal, to such a degree that the older artistic traditions were dying and being replaced by this new art from Europe.

As the perception and measurement of space affected the visual arts, so too did the perception and measurement of time affect music—though to a much lesser extent. At first sight, this selective rejection of Western music in the general process of Westernization is the reverse of what one would expect. Verbal culture, after all, would appear to be the most difficult, since in all its forms it requires either knowledge of a foreign language or the mediation of a translator. Yet in many ways it is precisely the literary and more generally verbal culture that has been the most accepted, and the best assimilated. Even among nonverbal cultural influences, we find the same contrast between the visual—artistic and architectural—influence, which on the whole has been very extensive, and the musical, which has been slow and limited. And in this we may perhaps discern an essential feature of Western civilization.

A distinguishing characteristic of Western music is polyphony, by harmony or counterpoint. This begins in its simplest form with the choir, in which matched voices sing different notes in a planned sequence to produce a combined effect; then comes the keyboard instrument, matching the ten fingers of the two hands, following different routes in a common purpose; and finally, the musical ensemble, from duets and trios to the full orchestra. Different performers play together, from different scores, producing a result that is greater than the sum of its parts.

With a little imagination one may discern the same feature in other aspects of Western culture—in democratic politics and in team games, both of which require the cooperation, in harmony if not in unison, of different performers playing different parts in a common purpose. In parliamentary politics and team games, there is a further cooperation in conflict—rival parties or teams, striving to defeat their opponents, but nevertheless acting under an agreed set of rules, and in an agreed interval of time. One may also detect the same feature in two distinctly Western literary creations—the novel, and still more, the theater. Both of these involve the combined activities of a number of different individuals—in the novel in imagination, in the theater in person—whose characters and interrelationships are seen to develop and change in the course of time. Such are the differences between the tale and the novel, the recitation and the theater, and—one might perhaps add—the autocrat and the assembly. The same qualities may be seen, in a more obvious form, in the work of the historian, and indeed distinguishes his writing from that of the chronicler or annalist.

All these involve some degree of harmonization—by the novelist or playwright, the party leader or team captain, the composer and conductor. The same applies, perhaps with even greater force, to modern scientific research, which is no longer the preserve of the lone genius, but has come to rely increasingly on teamwork and organization. Modern science has extended our capacity to observe and to measure both time and space to a previously inconceivable degree, extending the scale from the nanosecond to the light year.

Polyphony, in whatever form, requires exact synchronization. The ability to synchronize, to match times exactly, and for this purpose to measure times exactly, is an essential feature of modernity and therefore a requirement of modernization.

The precise measurement of passing time is of course a prerequisite of modern science and technology—both scientific research and working technology. It is also an essential characteristic, so obvious as usually to be taken for granted, of both private and public life in a modern society. The timetable—the tabulation of a sequence of events taking place at predetermined intervals, defined and demarcated with meticulous exactitude—is basic. In many ways the least dramatic and most powerful instrument of change in the whole process of modernization, it seems to have begun with the railway—the earliest form of organized public transport covering fixed distances at fixed times, and available to all who buy a ticket. The railway was followed by numerous other forms of public transport, covering ever greater distances at ever greater speeds. Before long, the Western world was crisscrossed by such lines of communication, and the timetable, indicating times of departure and arrival, became a feature of everyday life. The railway brought the timetable to the Middle East, and was followed by all the other modalities of modern transport and hence of modern life. Today the whole apparatus of modern communication, from telegraph through telephone to television, with more recent additions such as fax and Internet, is at the disposal of Middle-Eastern governments, and, increasingly, of those who oppose and seek to overthrow them.

Without timetables of one sort or another, neither society nor the economy could function, and the state would rapidly decline through confusion to chaos. Even such essential features of modern life as parades and demonstrations, political parties and business corporations, school curricula and the armed forces at all levels, from vast armies to simple infantry platoons, would be impossible.

The modern history of the Middle East, according to a convention accepted by most historians of the region, begins in 1798, when the French Revolution, in the persons of General Napoleon Bonaparte and his expedition, arrived in Egypt, and for the first time subjected one of the heartlands of Islam to the rule of a Western power and the direct impact of Western attitudes and ideas. Interestingly, this aspect of the French occupation was seen immediately in Istanbul, where the sultan, as suzerain of Egypt, was much concerned about the seditious effect of these ideas on his subjects. A proclamation was therefore prepared and distributed both in Turkish and in Arabic throughout the Ottoman lands, refuting the doctrines of revolutionary France. It begins: ". . . In the name of God, the merciful and the compassionate. O you who believe in the oneness of God, community of Muslims, know that the French nation (may God devastate their dwellings and abase their banners) are rebellious infidels and dissident evildoers. They do not believe in the oneness of the Lord of Heaven and Earth, nor in the mission of the intercessor on the Day of Judgement, but have abandoned all religions and denied the afterworld and its penalties. They do not believe in the Day of Resurrection and pretend that only the passage of time destroys us and that beyond this there is no resurrection and no reckoning, no examination and no retribution, no question and no answer."[10]

"The passage of time" is an allusion to the Qur'ān 45:23/24, which reads: "They [the unbelievers] say 'there is nothing in our life but this world. We die and we live and only time destroys us.' Of this they have no knowledge; they only guess." The word translated "time" is the Arabic *dahr*, one of many different Arabic words for time. It is usually used in the sense of passage or, often, duration of time. The term, *dahriyya*, followers of *dahr*, is the classical term used by Muslim theologians for materialism in its various forms. There is indeed an extensive philosophical and theological literature discussing the nature of time. Such discussions are of little relevance at the present day.

The clock and the timetable, the calendar and the program—these are the instruments by which modernity, itself a new and modern concept, is being introduced. By now, the whole world, including the Middle East, has so thoroughly accepted them that they are no longer recognized as of Western origin. The transformation of life through the introduction of the 24-hour day, and of devices to monitor and even to plan its passing, is enormous. In addition to timetables, it has made possible such things as schedules, agendas, programs, intervals, recesses, and, perhaps most difficult of all to assimilate, the making and keeping of appointments.

The last word on this may be left to a distinguished French writer who toured the Middle East in 1947: "I have made and I still make the most sincere efforts, during my travels in the East, to arrive late at the appointments which they were kind enough to give me and the time of which was always carefully discussed and finally agreed. I must admit that these virtuous attempts remain unsuccessful.

Wise and experienced men . . . sometimes said to me: 'Here the sky is too blue, the sun too hot. Why hurry? Why do injury to the sweetness of living? Here, everybody is late. The only thing is to join them. He who arrives at the appointed hour risks wasting his time, and that, after all, is not funny. Therefore, not too much precision. Strict exactitude has minor advantages, but is very inconvenient. It lacks suppleness, it lacks fantasy, it lacks cheerfulness, even dignity.'"[11]

7

Aspects of Cultural Change

In about 1830, a young British naval officer called Adolphus Slade was dining with friends on the shore of the Bosphorus and was rather surprised to hear the strains of a military band playing Rossini, coming from the direction of the Topkapı Palace. His interest aroused, he undertook some enquiries and made an interesting discovery: The band was formed, trained, and conducted by, as he said in the language of the time, a Sardinian.[1]

This alien presence in the palace was not as startling as might at first appear. The sultan at the time, Mahmud II, was engaged in a large-scale reform of the Ottoman armed forces, a necessity in order to survive in the modern world. The army was being reorganized, reequipped, more particularly rearmed. But that was not all. In addition to their new weaponry, the sultan provided his new-style army with Western-type uniforms and even with a brass band. Music, including military music, was of course old established, and Islamic civilization has a rich musical tradition of its own. Military bands are attested in the high Middle Ages, and figure prominently in the armies of the Ottoman Empire, both on parade and in battle. They consisted of drums and trumpets, sometimes in large numbers. By the eighteenth century the Turkish military music had become known in Europe, and even inspired some notable European imitations. But along with his new weapons and his new uniforms, Sultan Mahmud felt it appropriate to introduce new music. In all his reforms, he sought help from abroad—from the Prussians for the army, from the British for the navy, from the French for the bureaucracy. In the same spirit,

Figure 7-1
A Naval Battalion and Band. From the Library of Congress,
Sultan Abdul Hamid II's Photographic Albums.

he asked the Sardinian embassy in Istanbul to provide a bandmaster, to train and conduct—or should one say command?—his brass band.

In due course a bandmaster arrived. His name was Donizetti—Giuseppe Donizetti, the brother of the more famous Gaetano Donizetti, the composer. Signor Donizetti set to work and formed what was officially designated as the *Musiki-i Humayun-i Osmani*, the Imperial Ottoman Music—a military band in the Western style, playing Western instruments and of course Western music.[2]

This was different from all the other reforms, or at least from most of the other reforms. The primary purpose of the modernization was military. Defeat had made it clear even to the most conservatively reluctant that something was wrong and needed to be put right, and the sultan and his advisors set to work to create a new army. This meant, of course, a new officer corps, with new training and new weapons, and the infrastructure that was needed to support, train, equip and move this army.

All these were military choices, inevitably leading to political, economic, and social choices. They did not in themselves require cultural change. One could perhaps describe the introduction of Western-style uniforms as a cultural choice. The sultan had to re-equip and reorganize his army, but he didn't have to dress them in slacks and tunics and Sam Browne belts. But this had, one might argue, a military, perhaps a disciplinary, usefulness. A band playing Rossini, in contrast, is an unequivocally cultural choice; it is also the point where we can unhesitatingly speak of Westernization rather than modernization—two terms the content and meaning of which have been the subject of much argument.

Cultural change is Westernization; part of modernization, no doubt, but not, according to a widely held view, an essential part of it. It was possible, according to this view, to modernize without Westernizing; it was possible to have a modern army without Signor Donizetti and his brass band, to accept the weaponry and gadgetry of the West without being infected by its pernicious and corrupting culture.

It didn't seem to take very well—this musical Westernization. If one looks back to earlier times, there is practically no trace of any European cultural influence in the area of music, in spite of many centuries of contact between the Middle Eastern and Western worlds. We have a few, mostly negative, comments from Muslim visitors to Europe. One of the earliest comes from the tenth century: A certain envoy from Muslim Spain, Ibrāhīm ibn Ya'qūb, speaks of singing which he heard in Schleswig. He describes it as a "quite horrible sound, resembling the barking of dogs but more beast-like. . . . "[3]

We have occasional references by other visitors, most of them diplomats (who else would have taken the trouble to visit Europe?). Some of them make fleeting references to European musical performances— the Vienna Boys' Choir, the Paris Opera, but their comments relate to the spectacle and to the audience rather than to the actual music.[4]

There wasn't then much of a past for Signor Donizetti's brass band. What sort of a future did it have? Donizetti remained in Turkey, and we hear of him from time to time. He was of course given an officer's commission in the Ottoman forces; for a bandmaster that was necessary. Later he was promoted to Miralay (brigadier-general), and eventually, by a later sultan, made a pasha. Donizetti Pasha still appears from time to time in the records and at the end of the century we hear of him, by this time no doubt an old man, conducting an orchestra of harem ladies, escorted by eunuchs, for the entertainment of the sultan. He started apparently with quartets and quintets, and then with their help developed an orchestra in the palace.[5]

We hear some occasional references to Western music. During World War I, Turkey's German and Austrian allies brought musicians to perform, presumably for their own people there, but some performances were also given for Turkish Muslim audiences in or near the palace.[6]

Generally the reception of Western music in the Middle East has been remarkably limited. To this very day the Middle East—with the exception of some Westernized enclaves—remains a blank on the itinerary of the great international virtuosos as they go on their world tours. They go to Western and Eastern Europe, to North and South America, and now increasingly to South Asia and the Far East. Western art music is now listened to, performed, and composed in Japan, in China, and in India. It remains profoundly alien in most of the Middle East.

The visual impact is incomparably greater. Anyone who has been to Istanbul must at one time or another have visited the Great Bazaar. In the courtyard of the entrance to the Bazaar, there is a mosque—the Nuruosmaniye Mosque, completed in 1755. It is an Ottoman imperial mosque in the grand tradition—a single dome over a wide lateral extension of space, at first sight much resembling its predecessors, the great mosques of Sultans Mehmed, Süleyman, Selim, and the rest. But there is one rather interesting difference, and that is the Italian Baroque exterior decoration.

When a foreign influence appears in something as central to a culture as an imperial foundation and a cathedral-mosque, there is clearly some faltering of cultural self-confidence. Something is happening; something important. If we compare the cultural changes in music and in art, we must be struck by the fact that the second is far older, goes on for far longer, and is in every way more successful. A prized possession of National Gallery in London is a portrait of the Ottoman Sultan Mehmed II, the Conqueror of Constantinople, by the Italian artist Gentile Bellini. The painting is in London, not in Istanbul, because Sultan Mehmed's successor, the more pious Beyazid, disapproved of portraits and disposed of his father's collection. But Mehmed the Conqueror was neither the first nor the last Muslim ruler to indulge himself in this way. The Mamluk Sultan Qā'it Bay is reported to have had his portrait painted by a European artist. Later it became quite usual among Middle-Eastern monarchs to bring in Western, mostly Italian, artists. In time we find local artists, sometimes trained in Europe, painting portraits. Painting a portrait was obviously a new and radical departure in the cultural traditions of a region that has a very rich and distinctive artistic tradition of its own.

Donizetti, it would seem, was the first to try and introduce Western music. The Italian artist who helped build the Nuruosmaniye Mosque more than half a century earlier was not by any means the first. He and his employers had already some experience on which to build. Western influences can be seen at quite an early date even as far east as Iran, where miniature art shows awareness of European ideas and practices.

Architectural influence becomes very clear both in the structure and in the interior decoration of buildings. By the nineteenth century it is almost universal; the older artistic and architectural traditions were dying and being replaced by this new art from Europe.

Visual Westernization can be seen in a number of other ways. We see it for example in practical matters: coins and postage stamps. There had been coins in the Middle East for a very long time; now they looked different. European usage in the form of royal portraits—an outrage according to traditional Muslim ideas—shows the degree of cultural penetration. Stamps were of course entirely new; the stamp was in itself a Western innovation, but still more so the form of the stamp—whom it portrays, what it depicts.

One of the attractions of European art, and especially of portraiture, must have been a kind of realism and accuracy very different from the formal, stylized art of the traditional miniature. Portraits that were realistic likenesses had an obvious attraction; before very long they also proved useful for monarchs and others who could afford to pay for them and knew how to use them. The same attraction explains the rapid acceptance and widespread use of photography, again in spite of the Muslim ban on human images.

Clothes also show the influence of Western visual conceptions. Clothes of course serve a double purpose; on the one hand to keep out the cold and the damp, on the other as a recognition signal to indicate identity. When people change the clothes that they wear and adopt the clothes of another society, this represents a significant cultural choice, and was both adopted and resisted as such. The clothing reform began with the armies, almost all of which now wear uniforms of Western pattern. Even the armies of Libya and the Islamic Republic of Iran still wear Western-type uniforms just as they use Western-type weapons. Weapons are a military necessity; uniforms are, at least in some degree, a cultural choice; one might almost say a cultural submission.

Shoes and hats are particularly important. Shoes were seen by many Western travelers in the eighteenth and nineteenth centuries as one of the key distinctions between Middle-Eastern and Western habits. When somebody is being Westernized or, in Middle-Eastern terms, is becoming Frankish in his habits, the wearing of leather shoes or boots acquires an almost emblematic quality. The supreme emblem is of course the headgear, which can indicate religion, allegiance, and sometimes occupation, and crowns the wearer even in death, as the carved headstones in an old-style cemetery attest.

In many ways the most important vehicle of cultural influence is of course the word—language and more particularly translation. The three major cultural groups in the Middle East, the users of Arabic, Persian, and Turkish, had a vast and rich literature at their disposal in all three languages. The rise of Western power was followed at first very tentatively and in a very exploratory way, by the beginnings of translation of Western books.

It is interesting and instructive to compare the modern translation movement of European books, which we may date from its small beginnings in the sixteenth century, with its medieval precursor, the great movement of translation from Greek, and to a lesser extent from Persian, into classical Arabic in the Middle Ages. In the medieval movement, the criterion of choice was usefulness; they translated what was useful, that is to say primarily medicine, astronomy, chemistry, physics, mathematics, and also philosophy, which at that time was considered useful.

And that's all. They did not translate literature of any kind. In the vast bibliography of works translated in the Middle Ages from Greek into Arabic, we find no poets, no dramatists, not even historians. These were not useful and they were of no interest; they did not figure in the translation programs. This was clearly a cultural rejection: you take what is useful from the infidel; but you don't need to look at his absurd ideas or to try and understand his inferior literature, or to study his meaningless history.

A comparison with the Ottoman translation movement shows some resemblances, some differences. As before, the major criterion was usefulness. But their definition of what is useful was more strictly practical than was that of their medieval predecessors. We find no philosophy among the sixteenth-, seventeenth-, and eighteenth-century translations; philosophy was no longer regarded as useful. Everything that was worth having had already been translated, from the writings of Plato and Aristotle; the subsequent thoughts of infidels could not possibly have any value. The Ottomans translated some works on geography, which was of obvious practical importance to them; a certain amount of military literature, especially useful when one is modernizing one's army along Western lines; and one thing that was new and did not figure among the medieval translations, and that is history. For the Ottomans, philosophy was not useful, but history was. In this they show a marked difference from some modern trends in our own society.

Medieval Islam was an intensely historical-minded society, and produced a vast, rich, and varied historical literature. But medieval Muslims were not interested in non-Muslim history, nor in pre-Muslim history apart from some limited attention to the historical references in the Qur'ān. Until the Mongol conquests, they have virtually nothing to say about their neighbors in Asia, Africa, and Europe, and very little even about their own pagan ancestors. The inclusion of the Islamic lands in the vast Mongol Empire brought some awareness of other civilizations, but it was of limited effect and duration. The Ottoman Turks did show some mild interest in the history of their neighbors. We find for example a history of France from the mythical Faramond to the year 1572, translated into Turkish.[7] It could be useful to know something about the history of France. But the subject, it seems, was not very highly regarded. This translation survives in a single manuscript preserved in Leipzig; obviously it was not a runaway success in Ottoman reading circles. But it was one of a number, and later we find other books being translated, dealing with the history and also the geography of European countries. These become more numerous and more important as time goes on. The first Turkish printing press, which flourished in Istanbul in the first half of the eighteenth century, printed in all 17 books, of which a fair number were books on history.

The nineteenth century brought a considerable development in the movement of translation from Western languages into Turkish in Turkey and Egypt, then into Arabic in Egypt and Syria, finally into Persian in Persia and India. Egypt of course is an Arabic-speaking country, but its first modernizing ruler, Muḥammad ʿAlī Pasha (ruled

1805–1848), was an Ottoman of Albanian origin, and he and his top military and other officials were all Turkish-speaking. The printing press that he set up in Bulaq published the first important series of printed translations of European books into both Turkish and Arabic. Between 1822 and 1842, 243 books were printed in Cairo, the great majority translations, more than half of them into Turkish. Works on military and naval subjects, including both pure and applied mathematics, were translated into Turkish; works on medicine, veterinary science, and agriculture were mostly translated into Arabic—an interesting indication of the division of functions between the Turkish-speaking Ottoman elite from outside and the Arabic-speaking natives of Egypt. Significantly, the few historical books translated and printed at the Cairo press in this early period are all in Turkish. History, it seems, was seen either as useful, or elitist, or both. Of four historical books printed between 1829 and 1834, one is on Catherine the Great of Russia, the other three on Napoleon and his time. The publication of historical translations was not resumed in Cairo until 1841, when a translation—this time in Arabic—appeared, of Voltaire's history of Charles XII of Sweden. This concentration on biography is the more remarkable if one contrasts it with the almost complete lack of book-length royal biography in the very rich historiographic literature in Arabic, Persian, and Turkish. A translation of Machiavelli's *The Prince* into Arabic was made in 1825. According to a note on the manuscript, it was translated by a Christian priest by order of the Pasha.[8] For reasons at which one can only guess, it was not printed.

There is one important exception to the general lack of interest in belles lettres or literature of any kind; the theater. The theater had of course flourished in the Middle East in antiquity, but it disappeared after the Islamic expansion. Greek theater was associated with pagan rites and rituals, and had no place in an Islamic society.

After a long absence, the theater reappeared with the arrival of the Spanish Jews in the fifteenth and sixteenth centuries. They had had some experience of the theater in Spain, and they staged performances which their new Turkish compatriots, more particularly their Turkish rulers, found interesting. The beginnings of the return of theater,

of theatrical performances in this part of the world, can be dated precisely from the their coming, and they soon found disciples and imitators, gypsies for example, who were better able to perform in Turkish
than they were. Later, Greeks and more especially Armenians became involved in the theater. Eventually there was a development of
a Turkish equivalent of the Italian *commedia dell'arte*—the *Orta oyunu*,
a kind of impromptu play—which became extremely popular all over
Turkey. One of the themes was a version of *Othello*, a subject which
had obvious resonance and immediate comprehensibility.

The theater spread further east from Turkey toward Persia, where
the famous Shi'ite passion theater first appears at the end of the eighteenth and beginning of the nineteenth century. There is a common,
but probably erroneous impression that the *ta'ziye*, the passion play
on the martyrdom of Hussein, goes back to the roots of Shi'ism. If it
does, those roots are well concealed. We do not hear of these performances until the end of the eighteenth and the beginning of the nineteenth century, and it seems not unreasonable to connect it to the
revival of the theater by refugees from Europe and their various local
imitators.

A major innovation in the technology of culture, particularly the
technology of communication in words, was the introduction of printing.[9] Printing had been known in Turkey since the fifteenth century.
Gutenberg's work in Europe was duly recorded in the Turkish annals, and presses were introduced to the Ottoman realms at an early
date, with the authorization of the sultan, but only by minority communities. The first were the Jews, followed later by the Greeks and
Armenians. They were allowed to print in their own languages and
scripts but were strictly forbidden to print in the Arabic script. The
argument put forward at the time was that this, being the script in
which the Qur'ān was written, was sacred, and therefore printing it
would be a kind of desecration. Another possible factor was the vested
interest of the guild of calligraphers.

Ibrahim Müteferrika, helped by the son of a former Ottoman ambassador to France, was able to persuade the authorities to permit the
establishment of a press for the printing of books in Turkish and Arabic, in Arabic characters. Between 1729 when it was established, and

1742, when it was closed, this first Turkish printing press issued 17 books, most of them dealing with history, geography, and language.

After several abortive attempts by Ibrahim's staff to restart the press, two secretaries of the Sublime Porte bought it from Ibrahim Müteferrika's heirs and, with a *ferman* from the sultan, resumed printing in 1784. Significantly, they began production with a succession of Ottoman histories. These were followed by a work on grammar, and by three books on military topics. In 1796, with the death of its new owner, the press again closed down. Meanwhile printing had been resumed in 1795 in a state-sponsored printing press at the School of Engineering and Artillery. Thereafter, many printing presses were established in the Ottoman lands, printing in both Turkish and Arabic.

The development of Persian printing vividly illustrates the diverse influences shaping the cultural history of Iran. Woodblock printing was introduced into Iran as early as the thirteenth century by the Mongol rulers who used it, Chinese-style, to print paper money. Despite the threat of capital punishment for refusing to accept it, the mass of the population would have nothing to do with the paper money, and the attempt was abandoned. The first book printed in the Persian language was probably a Judaeo-Persian Pentateuch, in Hebrew characters, printed in Istanbul in 1594 and presumably intended for use by Persian-speaking Jews. The earliest printing presses actually in Iran were due to Christians—first Carmelite friars who brought a printing press with Arabic type from Rome, and later Armenians, who set up a press in Julfa, an Armenian suburb of Isfahan. Both of these were of short duration, and for the rest of the seventeenth, eighteenth and early-nineteenth centuries, such printed Persian books as existed were imported both from Europe, where books in the Persian language and script were printed in Leiden from 1639 onward, and from British-controlled India. The conventional date for the first book printed in Iran is 1817. As in Turkey, there was some resistance to this infidel device, but in the course of the nineteenth and still more the twentieth century the printing press became very much a part of life. An interesting comment on this process was made by Kemal Atatürk in his speech at the opening of the new law school in Ankara on November 5, 1925:

Think of the Turkish victory of 1453, the conquest of Constantinople, and its place in the course of world history. That same might and power which, in defiance of a whole world, made Istanbul forever the property of the Turkish people, was too weak to overcome the ill-omened resistance of the men of law and to receive in Turkey the printing press, which had been invented at about the same time. Three centuries of observation and hesitation were needed, of effort and energy expended for and against, before antiquated laws and their exponents would permit the entry of printing into our country.[10]

The role of Jews and Christians in the introduction and establishment of printing illustrates the growing importance of another category of intermediaries, the non-Muslim minorities in the Muslim states. In the Ottoman Empire this meant principally, in order of their emergence in this role, Jews, Greeks, and Armenians; in Iran, mostly Armenians.

With printing came cheap and accessible books and, in due course, newspapers, the most important agent of cultural influence until the introduction, in the present century, of radio, television, fax, the Internet, E-mail, and all the modern electronic apparatus, the full effects of which are yet to be seen.

All these are channels of verbal communication and verbal influence; the principal instrument of verbal communication is of course language. We see interesting changes, first in Turkish, then in other languages. The most obvious, the most easily recognizable indicators of cultural change are the loanwords borrowed from Europe along with the notions and objects that they designate. Thus for example the Turkish words for parliament and senate are *parlamento* and *senato*, both obviously Italian. It is significant that while the Turkish word for senate is *senato*, the Turkish word for senator is *senatör*. They heard about senates, in Venice and elsewhere, long before they encountered a senator, and by then French had replaced Italian as the most widely used European language in the Middle East. Similarly, the Arabic term for parliament is *barlamān*, clearly from the French *parlement*.

One could add a number of other cultural terms. Some are loanwords, recognizable from the language of origin; others are *calque*, loan translation, that is to say using an original indigenous word but giving that word a new meaning in imitation of another language. An obvious instance is the word for electricity—not a cultural term, but it will serve as an example. Our word electricity comes from the Greek word for amber, *ēlektron*; the Arabic word for electricity, *kahrabā'*, comes from the Arabic word for amber, simply following the same pattern of semantic evolution as the Western term.

Less obvious but more relevant are the loan translations of such words as "freedom," "country," "nation," "government," and "revolution." In most of the languages of Islam, this last has shed its former negative connotation of sedition, upheaval, disturbance, and has become the most acceptable title to legitimacy.

For a long time, works of literature were almost entirely missing from the translation programs from European into Middle-Eastern languages, but this began to change at the turn of the eighteenth/ nineteenth centuries. By that time, readers of virtually any European language had access, through translations, to a considerable body of Arabic and Persian and, to a lesser extent, Turkish literature; to works of history, poetry, belles lettres, and many other things. In contrast, literally nothing of European literature was available in Arabic, Persian, or Turkish: not Shakespeare, not Dante, nor any other European writer apart, as noted, from some historical works—and even those were few and limited. History primarily meant political and military history, much of it in the form of biography. There was no great interest in that, and none in anything else. Middle-Eastern readers knew for example nothing of the Renaissance and precious little even of the Reformation, despite its obvious relevance to the conduct of Ottoman foreign policy. A seventeenth-century Ottoman Muslim scholar, who wrote a treatise explaining Christianity to his Ottoman Muslim readers, knew far more about the Christological controversies of the early Byzantine church than he did about the Reformation or even about the schism between Constantinople and Rome. These were of no interest to scholars and readers, though the later divisions within Christendom were known and sometimes used by those responsible for Ottoman dealings with European states.

The first literary translation, or rather adaptation, was based on a work by a French orientalist called Pétis de la Croix. His book, *Les mille et un jours* (*A Thousand and One Days*), first published in 1710–1712, is a collection of pseudo-oriental tales, a pastiche of *The Thousand and One Nights*. This is a European book, but it was obviously more accessible to Middle-Eastern readers than others. A Turkish version was made in the late eighteenth century by a certain Ali Aziz (d. 1798), an Ottoman official who had served in more than one European capital and had acquired a knowledge of French. Ali Aziz's version is very free and includes some new stories situated in eighteenth-century Istanbul.

After that there is nothing for a while, and then we find the first translations. An early favorite was *Robinson Crusoe*, translated in 1812 and printed in Malta in 1835. Again, the attraction was the book's relative familiarity. *Robinson Crusoe* was influenced by an Arabic model, *Ḥayy ibn Yaqẓān*, by the medieval Arab philosopher Ibn Tufayl. An English translation by Simon Ockley was published in London in 1708, only a few years before the first publication of *Robinson Crusoe*. A second Arabic translation, by Buṭrus al-Bustānī, was published in the late 1850s. In 1864, a Turkish version of *Robinson Crusoe* appeared, translated from the Arabic. Another work that seems to have had special appeal was *Télémaque* (1699) by the French author Fénélon, in the familiar form of a guide for the education of a young prince. An Arabic translation by a Christian from Aleppo was prepared in Istanbul in 1812, and is preserved in manuscript in the Bibliothèque Nationale. It was never printed. A Turkish translation was published in 1862, followed by Arabic and Persian.

In the course of the nineteenth century, there was a gradual increase in translations. Naturally, books with an Arab or Islamic theme were more acceptable. Chateaubriand's *The Adventures of the Last of the Abencérages* was translated or adapted in Arabic at least five times, the earliest in 1864. Historical novels seem to have been popular; in particular Sir Walter Scott and Alexandre Dumas found both translators and imitators. *The Talisman* has a Middle-Eastern setting and paints an admiring picture of Saladin; *The Count of Monte Cristo* brings an Arabian Nights flavor to a Western tale of treasure, love, and vengeance.

A translation requires a translator, and a translator has to know both languages, the language from which he is translating and the language into which he is translating. Such knowledge, strange as it may seem, was extremely rare in the Middle East until comparatively late. There were very few Muslims who knew any Christian language; it was considered unnecessary, even to some extent demeaning. For interpreters, when needed for commerce, diplomacy, or war, they relied first on refugees and renegades from Europe and then, when the supply of these dried up, on Levantines. Both groups lacked either the interest or the capacity to do literary translations into Middle-Eastern languages. It was not until Middle-Easterners, first Christians, then others, attended Western schools in the region and studied in Western universities that we find people with both the desire and the ability to translate books from English or French or, much later, other languages, into Arabic or Persian or Turkish.

Of the three forms of cultural influence, the visual, the musical, and the literary, the third is by now the most thoroughly assimilated. The European forms of literature—the novel, the short story, the play, and the rest—are now completely adopted and absorbed. Great numbers of original writings of this type are being produced in all these countries and, more than that, have become the normal forms of literary self-expression. Even the very texture of language has been affected, and some modern writing in Middle-Eastern languages, especially in newspapers, reads like a literal translation from English or French.

One might also refer to cultural influence in pastimes. Board games, notably backgammon and chess, are of course very old in this part of the world, and probably came to the West either from or via the Middle East. Cards would be a Western contribution, but they are just another vice, not a significant cultural change. A really significant cultural change may be seen in the arena of sport. Sport was not unknown of course; there were large-scale enterprises like hunting, and individual competitions like wrestling. There appears to have been only one team sport: polo, and that was rare and aristocratic. The practice of team sports like football and basketball and the rest is purely Western, mostly English in origin. It was the English who invented football and its analogue—parliamentary politics. There are remarkable resemblances between the two and both obviously come from the same national genius. The adoption of competitive team games has so far been more successful in the Middle East than the adoption of parliamentary government.

Dining—as distinct from merely eating—is another Western "cultural" influence. We have fascinating descriptions of dinner parties at various stages in the process of acculturation; dining and partying and of course the very shocking business of gentlemen and ladies dining together, even dancing together. This brings expressions of shock and outrage from many nineteenth century and early twentieth century travelers from East to West.

During the centuries of Western impact on the Middle East, Western verbal culture was completely accepted and internalized. One would have thought that the verbal culture would be the most difficult since it requires either knowledge of a language or the mediation of a translator. Yet for some reason, it has been the most successful and the most accepted.

The nonverbal cultural influences show a contrast between the visual, including physical, which have been on the whole successful; and the musical, which has been remarkably unsuccessful, and indeed to this day Western musical influence is minimal in this region. It seems that science and music remain the last citadels of Western civilization that some non-Westerners have managed to penetrate but others, particularly in the Middle East, have not.

Many regions have undergone the impact of the West, and suffered a similar loss of economic self-sufficiency, of cultural authenticity, and in some parts also of political independence. But some time has passed since Western domination ended in all these regions, including the Middle East. In some of them, notably in East and South Asia, the resurgent peoples of the region have begun to meet and beat the West on its own terms—in commerce and industry, in the projection of political and even military power, and, in many ways most remarkable of all, in the acceptance and internalization of Western achievement, notably in science. The Middle East still lags behind.

We find an even more dramatic contrast in the arts—not just between the Middle East and other regions, but even between different arts within the Middle East. The impact of European painting and architecture (though not of course sculpture, which is excluded for religious reasons) goes back a long way. In the course of the eighteenth century, and even more in the nineteenth century, European visual culture, architecture, and interior decoration, even painting, became not only accepted but even dominant. In the late nineteenth and still more in the twentieth century even sculpture was sometimes used for the glorification of rulers.[11] The more traditional forms have virtually disappeared, except for an occasional rather self-conscious burst of neoclassicism.[12]

European literary influence, facing the barrier of language and the interposition of translators, took somewhat longer to penetrate. Yet by now Western literary forms and fashions are thoroughly assimilated. Such distinctively European vehicles as the novel and the play have become normal forms of literary self-expression in all the literary languages of the Middle East.

The ready acceptance of the visual and verbal arts makes the rejection of music the more remarkable. It was not for lack of trying. Sultan Mahmud II was not alone in his experiment with a brass band. Other rulers saw the relevance of Western music to Western drill, and hence to Western warfare. Even the Ayatollah Khomeini, who in general fiercely denounced the sinfulness and corruption of all kinds of music and of Western music in particular, was willing to make an exception for marches and anthems.

In Turkey, where Westernization as distinct from modernization has made most progress, Western music has won the widest acceptance and there are Turkish soloists, orchestras, and even composers in the Western style. But these address only a minority of the population, and elsewhere in the Middle East—except Israel—Western music, that is of course Western art music, falls on deaf ears. Latterly there has been some interest in pop music and rock music. It is too early to say what this may portend.

The contrast between visual and verbal acceptance and musical rejection is paralleled in other areas, as for example in the widespread cult, without the exercise, of freedom, and the almost universal holdings of elections, without choice.

It may help to understand these matters if we view them in a broader historical perspective. In such a perspective, cultural innovation is not and never has been the monopoly of any one region or people; the same is true of resistance to it. There has been much borrowing both ways, and disciples have not always been faithful to their models. Medieval Europe took its religion from the Middle East, as the modern Middle East took its politics from Europe. And just as some Europeans managed to create a Christianity without compassion, so did some Middle Easterners create a democracy without freedom.

In every era of human history, modernity, or some equivalent term has meant the ways, norms, and standards of the dominant and expanding civilization. Every dominant civilization has imposed its own modernity in its prime. The Hellenistic kingdoms, the Roman Empire, the medieval Christendoms, and Islam, as well as the ancient civilizations of India and China, all imposed their norms over a wide area and radiated their influence over a much broader one, far beyond their imperial frontiers. Islam was the first to make significant progress toward what it perceived as its universal mission, but modern Western civilization is the first to embrace the whole planet. Today, for the time being, as Atatürk recognized and as Indian computer scientists and Japanese high-tech companies appreciate, the dominant civilization is Western, and Western standards therefore define modernity.

There have been other dominant civilizations in the past; there will no doubt be others in the future. Western civilization incorporates many previous modernities—that is to say, it is enriched by the contributions and influences of other cultures that preceded it in leadership. It will itself bequeath a Western cultural legacy to other cultures yet to come.

Conclusion

In the course of the twentieth century it became abundantly clear in the Middle East and indeed all over the lands of Islam that things had indeed gone badly wrong. Compared with its millennial rival, Christendom, the world of Islam had become poor, weak, and ignorant. In the course of the nineteenth and twentieth centuries, the primacy and therefore the dominance of the West was clear for all to see, invading the Muslim in every aspect of his public and—more painfully—even his private life.

Modernizers—by reform or revolution—concentrated their efforts in three main areas: military, economic, and political. The results achieved were, to say the least, disappointing. The quest for victory by updated armies brought a series of humiliating defeats. The quest for prosperity through development brought, in some countries, impoverished and corrupt economies in recurring need of external aid, in others an unhealthy dependence on a single resource—fossil fuels. And even these were discovered, extracted, and put to use by Western ingenuity and industry, and doomed, sooner or later, to be exhausted or superseded—probably superseded, as the international community grows weary of a fuel that pollutes the land, the sea, and the air wherever it is used or transported, and puts the world economy at the mercy of a clique of capricious autocrats. Worst of all is the political result: The long quest for freedom has left a string of shabby tyrannies, ranging from traditional autocracies to new-style dictatorships, modern only in their apparatus of repression and indoctrination.

Many remedies have been tried—weapons and factories, schools and parliaments—but none achieved the desired result. Here and there they brought some alleviation, and even—to limited elements of the population—some benefit. But they failed to remedy or even to halt the deteriorating imbalance between Islam and the Western world.

There was worse to come. It was bad enough for Muslims to feel weak and poor after centuries of being rich and strong, to lose the leadership that they had come to regard as their right, and to be reduced to the role of followers of the West. The twentieth century, particularly the second half, brought further humiliations—the awareness that they were no longer even the first among the followers, but were falling ever further back in the lengthening line of eager and more successful Westernizers, notably in East Asia. The rise of Japan had been an encouragement, but also a reproach. The later rise of the other new Asian economic powers brought only reproach. The proud heirs of ancient civilizations had got used to hiring Western firms to carry out tasks that their own contractors and technicians were apparently not capable of doing. Now they found themselves inviting contractors and technicians from Korea—only recently emerged from Japanese colonial rule—to perform these same tasks. Following is bad enough; limping in the rear is far worse. By all the standards that matter in the modern world—economic development and job creation, literacy and educational and scientific achievement, political freedom and respect for human rights—what was once a mighty civilization has indeed fallen low.

"Who did this to us?" is of course a common human response when things are going badly, and there have been indeed many in the Middle East, past and present, who have asked this question. They found several different answers. It is usually easier and always more satisfying to blame others for one's misfortunes. For a long time, the Mongols were the favorite villains, and the Mongol invasions of the thirteenth century were blamed for the destruction of both Muslim power and Islamic civilization, and for what was seen as the ensuing weakness and stagnation. But after a while historians, Muslims and others, pointed to two flaws in this argument. The first was that some of the greatest cultural achievements of the Muslim peoples, notably in Iran, came after, not before, the Mongol invasions. The second, more difficult to accept but nevertheless undeniable, was that the

Mongols overthrew an empire that was already fatally weakened—indeed, it is difficult to see how the once mighty empire of the caliphs would otherwise have succumbed to a horde of nomadic horsemen riding across the steppes from East Asia.

The rise of nationalism—itself an import from Europe—produced new perceptions. Arabs could lay the blame for their troubles on the Turks who had ruled them for many centuries.[1] Turks could blame the stagnation of their civilization on the dead weight of the Arab past in which the creative energies of the Turkish people were caught and immobilized. Persians could blame the loss of their ancient glories on Arabs, Turks, and Mongols impartially.

The period of French and British paramountcy in much of the Arab world in the nineteenth and twentieth centuries produced a new and more plausible scapegoat—Western imperialism. In the Middle East, there have been good reasons for such blame. Western political domination, economic penetration, and—longest, deepest, and most insidious of all—cultural influence, had changed the face of the region and transformed the lives of its people, turning them in new directions, arousing new hopes and fears, creating new dangers and new expectations equally without precedent in their own cultural past.

But the Anglo-French interlude was comparatively brief and ended half a century ago; the change for the worse began long before their arrival and continued unabated after their departure. Inevitably, their role as villains was taken over by the United States, along with other aspects of the leadership of the West. The attempt to transfer the guilt to America has won considerable support, but for similar reasons remains unconvincing. Anglo-French rule and American influence, like the Mongol invasions, were a consequence, not a cause, of the inner weakness of Middle-Eastern states and societies. Some observers, both inside and outside the region, have pointed to the differences in the postimperial development of former British possessions—for example, between Aden in the Middle East and such places as Singapore and Hong Kong; or between the various lands that once made up the British Empire in India.

Another European contribution to this debate is anti-Semitism, and blaming "the Jews" for all that goes wrong. Jews in traditional Islamic societies experienced the normal constraints and occasional hazards of minority status. In most significant respects, they were better off under Muslim than under Christian rule, until the rise and spread of Western tolerance in the seventeenth and eighteenth centuries.

With rare exceptions, where hostile stereotypes of the Jew existed in the Islamic tradition, they tended to be contemptuous and dismissive rather than suspicious and obsessive. This made the events of 1948—the failure of five Arab states and armies to prevent half a million Jews from establishing a state in the debris of the British Mandate for Palestine—all the more of a shock. As some writers at the time observed, it was bad enough to be defeated by the great imperial powers of the West; to suffer the same fate at the hands of a contemptible gang of Jews was an intolerable humiliation. Anti-Semitism and its demonized picture of the Jew as a scheming, evil monster provided a soothing answer.

The earliest specifically anti-Semitic statements in the Middle East occurred among the Christian minorities, and can usually be traced back to European originals. They had limited impact, and at the time for example of the Dreyfus trial in France, when a Jewish officer was unjustly accused and condemned by a hostile court, Muslim comments usually favored the persecuted Jew against his Christian persecutors. But the poison continued to spread, and from 1933 Nazi Germany and its various agencies made a concerted and on the whole remarkably successful effort to promote and disseminate European style anti-Semitism in the Arab world. The struggle for Palestine greatly facilitated the acceptance of the anti-Semitic interpretation of history, and led some to blame all evil in the Middle East and indeed in the world on secret Jewish plots. This interpretation has pervaded much of the public discourse in the region, including education, the media, and even entertainment.

Another view of the Jewish component, based in reality rather than fantasy, may be more instructive. The modern Israeli state and society were built by Jews who came from Christendom and Islam; that is, on the one hand from Europe and the Americas, on the other from the Middle East and North Africa. Judaism, or more broadly Jewishness, is a religion in the fullest sense—a system of belief and worship, a morality and a way of life, a complex of social and cultural values and habits. But until comparatively recent times Jews had no political role, and even in recent times that role is limited to a few countries. There is therefore no specifically Jewish political and societal culture or tradition. Ancient memories are too remote, recent experience too brief, to provide them. Between the destruction of the ancient Jewish kingdom and the creation of the modern Jewish republic, Jews were a part—one might say a subculture—of the larger societies in which they live, and even their communal organizations and usages inevitably reflected the structures and usages of those societies. For the last 14 centuries, the overwhelming majority of Jews lived in either the Christian or Islamic world, and were in many respects a component in both civilizations. Inevitably, the Jews who created Israel brought with them many of the political and societal standards and values, the habits and attitudes of the countries from which they came: on the one hand, what we have become accustomed to call the Judaeo-Christian tradition, on the other, what we may with equal justification call the Judaeo-Islamic tradition.

In present-day Israel these two traditions meet and, with increasing frequency, collide. Their collisions are variously expressed, in communal, religious, ethnic, even party-political terms. But in many of their encounters what we see is a clash between Christendom and Islam, oddly represented by their former Jewish minorities, who reflect, as it were in miniature, both the strengths and the weaknesses of the two civilizations of which they had been part. The conflict, coexistence, or combination of these two traditions within a single small state, with a shared religion and a common citizenship and allegiance, should prove illuminating. For Israel, this issue may have an existential significance, since the survival of the state, surrounded, outnumbered and outgunned by neighbors who reject its very right to exist, may depend on its largely Western-derived qualitative edge.

An argument sometimes adduced is that the cause of the changed relationship between East and West is not a Middle-Eastern decline but a Western upsurge—the Discoveries, the scientific movement, the technological, industrial, and political revolutions that transformed the West and vastly increased its wealth and power. But these comparisons do not answer the questions; they merely restate it—Why did the discoverers of America sail from Spain and not a Muslim Atlantic port, where such voyages were indeed attempted in earlier times?² Why did the great scientific breakthrough occur in Europe and not, as one might reasonably have expected, in the richer, more advanced, and in most respects more enlightened realm of Islam?

A more sophisticated form of the blame game finds its targets inside, rather than outside the society. One such target is religion, for some specifically Islam. But to blame Islam as such is usually hazardous, and rarely attempted. Nor is it very plausible. For most of the Middle Ages, it was neither the older cultures of the Orient nor the newer cultures of the West that were the major centers of civilization and progress, but the world of Islam in the middle. It was there that old sciences were recovered and developed and new sciences created; there that new industries were born and manufactures and commerce expanded to a level previously without precedent. It was there, too, that governments and societies achieved a degree of freedom of thought and expression that led persecuted Jews and even dissident Christians to flee for refuge from Christendom to Islam. The medieval Islamic world offered only limited freedom in comparison with modern ideals and even with modern practice in the more advanced democracies, but it offered vastly more freedom than any of its predecessors, its contemporaries and most of its successors.

The point has often been made—if Islam is an obstacle to freedom, to science, to economic development, how is it that Muslim society in the past was a pioneer in all three, and this when Muslims were much closer in time to the sources and inspiration of their faith than they are now? Some have indeed posed the question in a different form—not "What has Islam done to the Muslims?" but "What have the Muslims done to Islam?," and have answered by laying the blame on specific teachers and doctrines and groups.

For those nowadays known as Islamists or fundamentalists, the failures and shortcomings of the modern Islamic lands afflicted them because they adopted alien notions and practices. They fell away from authentic Islam, and thus lost their former greatness. Those known as modernists or reformers take the opposite view, and see the cause of this loss not in the abandonment but in the retention of old ways, and especially in the inflexibility and ubiquity of the Islamic clergy. These, they say, are responsible for the persistence of beliefs and practices that might have been creative and progressive a thousand years ago, but are neither today. Their usual tactic is not to denounce religion as such, still less Islam in particular, but to level their criticism against fanaticism. It is to fanaticism, and more particularly to fanatical religious authorities, that they attribute the stifling of the once great Islamic scientific movement, and, more generally, of freedom of thought and expression.[3]

A more usual approach to this theme is to discuss not religion in general, but a specific problem: the place of religion and of its professional exponents in the political order. For these, a principal cause of Western progress is the separation of church and state and the creation of a civil society governed by secular laws. For others, the main culprit is Muslim sexism, and the relegation of women to an inferior position in society, thus depriving the Islamic world of the talents and energies of half its people, and entrusting the crucial early years of the upbringing of the other half to illiterate and downtrodden mothers. The products of such an education, it was said, are likely to grow up either arrogant or submissive, and unfit for a free, open society. However one evaluates their views, the success or failure of secularists and feminists will be a major factor in shaping the Middle-Eastern future.

Some have sought the causes of this painful asymmetry in a variety of factors—the exhaustion of precious metals, coinciding with the discovery and exploitation by Europe of the resources of the new world; inbreeding, due to the prevalence of cousin marriage, especially in the countryside; the depredations of the goat that, by stripping the bark off trees and tearing up grass by the roots, turned once fertile lands into deserts. Others point to the disuse of wheeled vehicles in the pre-modern Middle East, variously explained as a cause or as a symptom of what went wrong.[4] Familiar in antiquity, they became rare in the medieval centuries, and remained so until they were reintroduced under European influence or rule. Western travelers in the Middle East note their absence; Middle-Eastern travelers in the West note their presence.

In a sense, this was a symptom of a bigger problem. A cart is large and, for a peasant, relatively costly. It is difficult to conceal and easy to requisition. At a time and place where neither law nor custom restricted the powers of even local authorities, visible and mobile assets were a poor investment.[5] The same fear of predatory authority—or neighbors—may be seen in the structure of traditional houses and quarters: the high, windowless walls, the almost hidden entrances in narrow alleyways, the careful avoidance of any visible sign of wealth. This much is clear—the advent of paved roads and wheeled vehicles in modern times brought no alleviation of the larger problems.

Some of the solutions that once commanded passionate support have been discarded. The two dominant movements in the twentieth century were socialism and nationalism. Both have been discredited, the first by its failure, the second by its success and consequent exposure as ineffective. Freedom, interpreted to mean independence, was seen as the great talisman that would bring all other benefits. The overwhelming majority of Muslims now live in independent states, which have brought no solutions to their problems. The bastard offspring of both ideologies, national socialism, still survives in a few states that have preserved the Nazi Fascist style of dictatorial government and indoctrination, the one through a vast and ubiquitous security apparatus, the other through a single all-powerful party. These regimes too have failed every test except survival, and have brought none of the promised benefits. If anything, their infrastructures are even more antiquated than the others, their armed forces designed primarily for terror and repression.

At the present day two answers to this question command widespread support in the region, each with its own diagnosis of what is wrong, and the corresponding prescription for its cure. The one, attributing all evil to the abandonment of the divine heritage of Islam, advocates a return to a real or imagined past. That is the way of the Iranian Revolution and of the so-called fundamentalist movements and regimes in other Muslim countries. The other way is that of secular democracy, best embodied in the Turkish Republic founded by Kemal Atatürk.

Meanwhile the blame game—the Turks, the Mongols, the imperialists, the Jews, the Americans—continues, and shows little sign of abating. For the governments, at once oppressive and ineffectual, that rule much of the Middle East, this game serves a useful, indeed an essential purpose—to explain the poverty that they have failed to alleviate and to justify the tyranny that they have intensified. In this way they seek to deflect the mounting anger of their unhappy subjects against other, outer targets.

But for growing numbers of Middle Easterners it is giving way to a more self-critical approach. The question "Who did this to us?" has led only to neurotic fantasies and conspiracy theories. The other question—"What did we do wrong?"—has led naturally to a second question: "How do we put it right?" In that question, and in the various answers that are being found, lie the best hopes for the future.

The worldwide exposure given to the views and actions of Osama bin Laden and his hosts the Taliban has provided a new and vivid insight into the eclipse of what was once the greatest, most advanced, and most open civilization in human history.

To a Western observer, schooled in the theory and practice of Western freedom, it is precisely the lack of freedom—freedom of the mind from constraint and indoctrination, to question and inquire and speak; freedom of the economy from corrupt and pervasive mismanagement; freedom of women from male oppression; freedom of citizens from tyranny—that underlies so many of the troubles of the Muslim world. But the road to democracy, as the Western experience amply demonstrates, is long and hard, full of pitfalls and obstacles.

If the peoples of the Middle East continue on their present path, the suicide bomber may become a metaphor for the whole region, and there will be no escape from a downward spiral of hate and spite, rage and self-pity, poverty and oppression, culminating sooner or later in yet another alien domination; perhaps from a new Europe reverting to old ways, perhaps from a resurgent Russia, perhaps from some

new, expanding superpower in the East. If they can abandon griev-
ance and victimhood, settle their differences, and join their talents,
energies, and resources in a common creative endeavor, then they
can once again make the Middle East, in modern times as it was in
antiquity and in the Middle Ages, a major center of civilization. For
the time being, the choice is their own.

Afterword

The core of this book was a series of three public lectures given at the Institut für die Wissenschaften vom Menschen in Vienna in September 1999 and published by them, in German translation, under the title *Kultur and Modernisierung im Nahen Osten*, in 2001. The Vienna lectures, extensively recast and re-written, constitute the basis of Chapters 1–3. Later chapters include passages from other previous publications: an article published in the *Revue de Métaphysique*, 1995, and three contributions—the first to the International Congress of Historical Sciences, Madrid (1992), the second and third to colloquia held in Strasbourg (1980) and Castel Gandolfo (1998). All three were published in the proceedings of these meetings. My thanks are due to the organizers of these various events for giving me the opportunity to formulate my views and put them before an informed audience. I would also like to express my thanks to my editor, Ms. Susan Ferber, for many constructive suggestions; to Mr. Eli Alshech, a graduate student at Princeton, for help of various kinds in the processes of research and exposition, and, once again, to my assistant Ms. Annamarie Cerminaro, for the care and skill with which she tended my manuscript from the first drafts to the final published version.

Bernard Lewis,
2001

Notes

INTRODUCTION

1. See Abdulhak Adnan, *La Science chez les Turcs ottomans* (Paris: 1939), pp. 87, 98–9.

2. *The Turkish Letters of Ogier Ghiselin de Busbecq, Imperial Ambassador at Constantinople 1554–1562*, translated from the Latin by Edward Seymour Forster (Oxford: 1927), p. 112.

3. *The Poems of James VI of Scotland*, ed. J. Craigie, vol. i (Edinburgh: 1955), pp. 197 ff.

4. Cited in Michel Lesure, *Lépante: la crise de l'empire ottoman* (Paris: 1972), p. 180.

5. Ibrahim Peçevi, *Tarih* [History], vol. 1, Istanbul 1281/1864, pp. 498–9. See Andrew C. Hess, "The Battle of Lepanto," *Past and Present*, vol. 57 (November 1972): 53–73.

6. This word occurs in Hungarian and several Slavic languages, and apparently derived from Charlemagne in the same way that "Czar" and "Kaiser" derive from Caesar.

7. On the tradition that this title was conceded to the French King Francis I by the Ottoman Sultan Süleyman the Magnificent, see Bernard Lewis, *The Political Language of Islam* (Chicago: 1988), pp. 98, 153–4.

8. Lûtfi Pasha, *Asafname*, edited with a German translation by Rudolf Tschudi (Berlin: 1910), pp. 32–3; translation, pp. 26–7.

9. The observations of Ömer Talib, written on the margins of a manuscript of the *Tarih al-Hind al-Garbi*, (see pp. 37–39 and note 4) in Ankara (Maarif Library 10024), were published by A. Zeki Velidi Togan, *Bugünkü Türkeli (Turkistan' ve Yakm Tarihi*, vol. i (1947), p. 127, translated in B. Lewis, *The Emergence of Modern Turkey*, new edition (New York: 2001), p. 28, note 11.

10. On this episode see Saffet, "Bir Osmanlı filosunun Sumatra seferi," in *Tarih-i Osmani Encümeni Mecmuası*, vol. 10 (1327 A.H.), Istanbul, 1329 A.H., pp. 604–614, 678–683; Halil Inalcik with Donald Quatert (eds.), *An Eco-*

nomic and Social History of the Ottoman Empire 1306–1914 (Cambridge: 1994), pp. 327–31 and 345–7. See further Salih Özbaran, "The Ottoman Turks and the Portuguese," *Journal of Asian History*, vol. vi/i (1972): 48–87.

11. For a recent study, see Şevket Pamuk, *A Monetary History of the Ottoman Empire* (Cambridge: 1999), especially chapters 7 and after.

12. Sılıhdar Fındıklı Mehmed, *Tarih* (Istanbul: 1928), vol. II, p. 87.

13. Cited in *Ahmed Refik: Hayatı, Seçme Şiir ve Yazıları*, ed. Reşad Ekrem Koçu (Istanbul: 1938), p. 101. "Wash" refers of course to the ritual ablution before prayer.

CHAPTER 1

1. Faik Reşit Unat, "Ahmet III devrine ait bir islahat takriri: Muhayyel bir mülâkatın zabıtları," *Tarih Vesikaları*, vol. i (1941): 107–121.

2. Cited in V. J. Parry, "La Manière de Combattre," in *War, Technology and Society in the Middle East*, V. J. Parry and M. E. Yapp, eds. (London: 1975), p. 252, note 2.

3. In Article XIII, the Sublime Porte promises to use "the sacred title Empress of all the Russias in all documents and public letters, and to do so in all cases in the Turkish language." The text of the treaty then spells out the Turkish form, rendering "Empress" by "Padishah"—a title already conceded to the Holy Roman Emperor. The treaty was written in Italian, the diplomatic language of the time, at least in the eastern Mediterranean area. In the Italian text, the ruler of the Ottomans, whose title was Padishah, is called "Padischag." Only a Russian—certainly neither an Italian nor a Turk—would replace "h" by "g." The Italian text of the treaty of Küçük Kaynarca is found in G. G. de Martens, *Recueil de Traités*, vol. IV (1761–1790 supplement) (Göttingen: 1798), no. 71, pp. 606–638; 2nd ed., vol. IV (1771–1779) (Göttingen: 1817), pp. 287–322.

4. See Bernard Lewis, "From Babel to Dragomans," in *Proceedings of the British Academy*, vol. 101 (1999): 37–54.

5. Lûtfi Pasha, *Asafname*, edited with a German translation by Rudolf Tschudi, Berlin 1910.

6. *Risale-i Koçu Bey* (Istanbul: 1277/1860), and several subsequent editions. German translation by W. F. A. Behrnauer, in *Zeitschrift der Deutschen Morgenländischen Gesellschaft*, vol. XI (1861): 272–332. On these and other similar works see Virginia H. Aksan, "Ottoman Political Writing, 1768–1808," *International Journal of Middle Eastern Studies*, vol. 25 (1993): 53–69; and Bernard Lewis, "Ottoman Observers of Ottoman decline," *Islamic Studies* (Karachi), vol. I, (1962): 71–87; reprinted in idem, *Islam in History: Ideas, People and Events in the Middle East*, rev. ed. (Chicago: 1993), pp. 209–222.

7. Lûtfi Pasha, pp. 32–3; translation, pp. 26–7.

8. For two studies of these, the one in an Islamic, the other in a European context, see Bartolomé Bennassar and Lucile Bennassar, *Les chrétiens d'Allah: l'histoíre extraordinaire des renégats, XVIᵉ–XVIIᵉ siècles* (Paris: 1989); and Lucetta Scaraffia, *Rinnegati: per una storia dell'identità occidentale* (Rome-Bari: 1993).

9. On these and other Muslim envoys to Europe, see B. Lewis, *The Muslim Discovery of Europe* (New York: 1982), rev. 1994, s.vv.*; Carter Vaughn Findley, "État et droit dans la pensée politique ottomane: droits de l'homme o Rechtsstaat? À propos de deux relations d'ambassade," in *Études Turques et Ottomanes*, vol. IV (Paris: December 1995), 39–50; Virginia H. Aksan, *An Ottoman Statesman in War and Peace: Ahmed Resmi Efendi, 1700–1783* (Leiden: 1995).

10. On Ratib Efendi see Carter Vaughn Findley, "Ebu Bekir Ratib's Vienna Embassy Narrative: Discovering Austria or Propagandizing for Reform in Istanbul?" in *Wiener Zeitschrift für die Kunde des Morgenlandes*, vol. 85 (Vienna: 1995), pp. 41–80; and J. M. Stein, "An Eighteenth-Century Ottoman Ambassador Observes the West: Ebu Bekir Ratip Efendi Reports on the Habsburg System of Roads and Posts," in *Archivum Ottomanicum*, vol. X (Wiesbaden: 1985) [1987]: 219–312.

11. On the introduction and history of printing in the Middle East, see pp. 142–144.

12. *Uṣūl al-ḥikam fī niẓām al-umam*, Istanbul 1145/1732. A French translation by Baron Reviczki, *Traité de la tactique*, was published in Vienna in 1769.

13. See *Mémoires du Baron de Tott sur les Turcs et les Tartares*, 4 vols. (Maestricht:1785).

CHAPTER 2

1. Paolo Preto, *Venezia e i Turchi* (Florence: 1975), p. 132.

2. Abu'l 'Abbās Aḥmad ibn Yaḥyā al-Wansharīsī, "Asnā al-matājir fi bayān aḥkām man ghalaba 'ala waṭanihi al-Naṣārā wa-lam yuhājir," ed. Ḥusayn Mu'nis, *Revista del Instituto Egipcio de Estudios Islamicos en Madrid*, vol. V (1957), 129–191; see further B. Lewis, "Legal and Historical Reflections on the Position of Muslim Populations under non-Muslim Rule," *Journal: Institute of Muslim Minority Affairs*, vol. 13:1 (January 1992): 1–16, reprinted in idem, *Islam and the West* (New York-Oxford: 1993), pp. 43–57.

3. On this map see Svat Soucek in *The History of Cartography*, II, 1, *Cartography in the traditional Islamic and South Asian societies*, J. B. Harley and David Woodward, eds. (Chicago: 1992), pp. 269–272. See also Andrew C. Hess, "Piri Reis and the Ottoman response to the voyages of discovery," *Terrae Incognitae*, vol. 6 (1974): 19–37.

4. An edition in 500 copies was one of the first books printed at the Müteferrika press. (See p. 142) On this book see Thomas D. Goodrich, *The Ottoman Turks and the New World: a study of "Tarih-i Hind-i garbi" and Sixteenth century Ottoman Americana* (Wiesbaden: 1990).

5. Haskell Isaacs, "European influences in Islamic medicine, " in *Mashriq: Proceedings of the Eastern Mediterranean Seminar, University of Manchester 1977–1978* (Manchester: 1980).

6. Abdülhak Adnan [Adıvar], *La Science chez les Turcs Ottomans* (Paris: 1939), pp. 112–3.

7. See Fatma Müge Göcek, *Rise of the Bourgeoisie, Demise of Empire: Ottoman Westernization and Social Change* (New York-Oxford: 1996), p. 106.

8. On traditional and modern diplomacy in the Middle East, see *Encyclopædia of Islam*, 2nd edition, svv. "Elçi" and "Safīr," where further references are given.

9. J. Th. Zenker, *Bibliotheca Orientalis: Manual de Bibliographie orientale* (Leipzig: 1846), lists 1859 printed books, including 201 volumes devoted to poets and poetry (65 Arabic, 102 Persian, 34 Turkish), most of them editions and translations of texts.

10. Adnan, *La Science chez les Turcs Ottomans*, p. 57.

11. On Hoca Ishak Efendi, see Ekmeleddin Ihsanoğlu, *Başhoca Ishak Efendi: Türkiyede modern bilimin öncüsü* (Ankara: 1989).

12. For an example, see V. J. Parry, "La Manière de Combattre," p. 250.

13. Enver Ziya Karal, *Halet Efendinin Paris Büyük Elçiliği 1802–6* (Istanbul: 1940), pp. 32–3.

14. Perhaps because of the relative accessibility of the documentation, the economic aspect of Western impact has received far more attention than the social, cultural, and to a lesser extent even the political aspects. See Donald Quataert, *Social Disintegration and Popular Resistance in the Ottoman Empire, 1881–1908: Reactions to European Economic Penetration* (New York: 1983); and Şevket Pamuk, *The Ottoman Empire and European Capitalism, 1820–1913; Trade, Investment and Production* (Cambridge: 1987).

15. *Takvim-i Vekayi (Moniteur Ottoman)*, vol. 1 Jumada I 1247/14 May 1832.

16. *Tarih-i Naima* (Istanbul n.d.), vol. III, pp. 69–70 and vol. IV, p. 94.

17. On these, see B. Lewis, "Serbestiyet," *Journal of the Faculty of Economics of the University of Istanbul*, vol. 41 (1983): 47–52; idem. *Islam in History*, pp. 323–36.

18. Cited in Ahmed Jevdet Pasha, *Tarih*, vol. VI (Istanbul: 1309 A.H.), pp. 394–401: English translation in B. Lewis, "The Impact of the French Revolution on Turkey," *Journal of World History*, vol. i, (1953): 121–2, revised

version in G. S. Métraux and F. Crouzet (eds.), *The New Asia: Readings in the History of Mankind* (New York: 1965), pp. 47–50.

19. Şanizade, *Tarih*, vol. iv (Istanbul: 1291/1874), pp. 2–3.

20. Sadık Rıfat Pasha, *Muntehabat-i Asar* (Istanbul: n.d.), p. 4; another version in Abdurrahman Şeref, *Tarih Musahebeleri* (Istanbul: 1340/1922), p. 125.

CHAPTER 3

1. Evliya Çelebi, *Seyahatname* (Istanbul: 1928), vol. VII, pp. 318–9; German translation by R. F. Kreutel, *Im Reiche des goldenen Apfels* (Graz: 1957), pp. 194–5.

2. Mustafa Hatti Efendi, *Viyana Sefaretnamesi*, ed. Ali Ibrahim Savaş (Ankara: 1999), pp. 37–8. The text of Hatti's report was first published in the chronicle of Izzi, *Tarih-i Izzi* (Istanbul: 1199/1784), p. 190 ff.

3. Cited in *Tarih-i Cevdet* (Istanbul: 1309/1892) vol. IV, p. 355.

4. Aḥmad ibn al-Mahdī, *Natījat al-Ijtihād fī 'l-Muhādana wa'l-jihād*, ed. Alfredo Bustani (Larache [Morocco]: 1941), p. 12.

5. See for example Qur'ān V:119, where Jesus himself rejects this idea, in answer to a question from God: "Did you tell people: 'Worship me and my mother as gods apart from God?'" To this Jesus replied with an unequivocal denial.

6. Cited by M. Şükrü Hanioğlu, "Transformation of the Ottoman Intelligentsia and the idea of Science," in *Anuarul Institutului de Istorie si Arheologie "A.D. Xenopol,"* vol. XXIV/2 (Jassy: 1987), pp. 29–34.

7. English translation in B. Lewis, *A Middle East Mosaic: Fragments of Life, Letters and History* (New York: 2000), p. 192.

8. See *EI²*, *s.v.*, "Ḳāsim Amīn." His first book, *Taḥrīr al-mar'a* (Liberation of Woman) was published in Cairo in 1899; his second, *Al-Mar'a al-Jadīda* (The New Woman) in 1901. An English translation by Samiha Sidhom Peterson was published in Cairo in 2000.

9. For some examples see *Islam and Revolution: Writings and Declarations of Imam Khomeini*, translated and annotated by Hamid Algar (Berkeley: 1981).

10. Long neglected, the position of women in Islam has in recent years formed the topic of an extensive literature, both scholarly and polemical, much of it by Muslim women. The following is a very short selection, excluding books dealing with only one country: Lois Beck and Nikkie Keddie, eds., *Women in the Muslim World* (Cambridge, Mass.: 1978); Juliette Minces, *La femme dans le monde arabe* (Paris: 1980); Fatma Mernissi, *Beyond the Veil: Male-Female Dynamics in Modern Muslim Society*, rev. ed. (Bloomington: 1988); Hisham Sharabi, *Neopatriarchy: a Theory of Distorted Change in Arab Society*

(New York-Oxford: 1988); Margot Badran and Miriam Cooke, eds., *Opening the Gates: a Century of Arab Feminist Writing* (Bloomington: 1990); Nikki Keddie and Beth Baron, eds., *Women in Middle Eastern History: Shifting Boundaries in Sex and Gender* (New Haven: 1991); Bouthaina Shaaban, *Both Right and Left Handed: Arab Women talk about their lives* (Bloomington: 1991); Wiebke Walther, *Women in Islam* (Princeton: 1993); Fatma Müge Göçek and Shiva Balaghi, eds., *Reconstructing Gender in the Middle East: tradition, identity and power* (New York: 1994); Madeline C. Zilfi, ed., *Women in the Ottoman Empire: Middle Eastern Women in the Early Modern Era* (Leiden: 1997).

11. Mustafa Sami, *Avrupa Risalesi* (Istanbul: 1256 A.H.), pp. 26, 35–36; translation in Hanioğlu, p. 30.

12. *Âsâr-i Rıfat Paşa* (Istanbul: 1275 A.H.), pp. 10–11; translation in Hanioğlu, p. 31.

13. On Ibn al-Nafīs see Max Meyerhof, *Ibn al-Nafīs und seine Theorie des Lungenkreislaufs*, in *Quellen und Studien zur Geschichte der Naturwissenschaften*, vol. iv (Berlin: 1933); Gaston Wiet, "Ibn al-Nafīs et la circulation pulmonaire," *Journal Asiatique* (1956): 95–100; J. Schacht, "Ibn al-Nafīs, Servetus and Colombo," *al-Andalus*, vol. xxii (1937): 317–36; *EI²*, *s.v.*

14. See Aydın Sayılı, *The Observatory in Islam and its Place in the General History of the Observatory* (Ankara: 1960), pp. 289 ff.

15. See pp. 128–129 and 133–136.

CHAPTER 4

1. G. Young, *Corps de droit ottoman*, vol. II (Oxford: 1903), pp. 171–172.

2. Young, vol. II, pp. 172–174 and 180–181.

3. Young, vol. II, pp. 175ff.

4. M. Bompard, *Législation de Tunisie* (Paris: 1888), p. 398.

5. Ahmad ibn Khālid al-Nāṣirī, *Kitāb al-Istiqṣā'*, vol. V (Casablanca: 1955), pp. 131ff. On an earlier discussion of the illegal enslavement of black Muslims, by an African jurist, see *Mi'rāj al-Ṣu'ūd: Ahmad Baba's replies on slavery*, annotated and translated by John Hunwick and Fatima Karrak (Rabat: 2000), and Mahmoud A. Zouber, *Ahmad Baba de Timboktou (1556–1627): sa vie et son œuvre* (Paris: 1977), pp. 129–146.

6. On slavery, see the article "'Abd" by R. Brunschvig, in *Encyclopaedia of Islam*, 2nd edition (*EI²*) and Hans Müller, "Sklaven" in *Handbuch der Orientalistik*, ed. B. Spuler, Part I, *Der Nahe und der Mittlere Osten*, vol. VI, *Geschichte der Islamischen Länder*, Section 551, *Wirtschaftsgeschichte des Vorderen Orients in Islamischer Zeit*, Part I (Leiden and Cologne: 1977), pp. 54–83, with an extensive bibliography. See also B. Lewis, *Race and Slavery in the*

Middle East (New York: 1990); Ehud R. Toledano, *The Ottoman Slave Trade and its Suppression* (Princeton, New Jersey: 1982). For a remarkable debate on slavery and the slave trade in Africa and Arabia in the mid-twentieth century, see *The Parliamentary Debates (Hansard) Fifth Series—Volume CCXXV House of Lords Official Report: Seventh Volume . . . from Monday, 11ᵗʰ July, 1960 to Thursday, 27ᵗʰ October, 1960*, Cols. 333–356.

7. Louis Frank, *Mémoire sur le commerce des nègres au Kaire* (Paris: 1802), pp. 32–35. English translation by Michel Le Gall in *Princeton Papers*, vol. VII, "Slavery in the Islamic Middle East," edited by Shaun E. Marmon (1999), pp. 69 ff.

8. Harold Motzki, *Dimma und Egalité, Die nichtmuslimischen Minderheiten Ägyptens in der zweiten Hälfte des 18. Jahrhunderts und die Expedition Bonapartes (1798–1801), Studien zum Minderheitenproblem im Islam 5* (Bonn: 1979), pp. 263ff. and 324ff.

9. R. H. Davison, "Turkish attitudes concerning Christian-Muslim equality in the nineteenth century," *American Historical Review*, vol. LIX (1953–1954): 844–864.

10. The text of these and other Ottoman reform edicts may be found in G. Aristarchi, *Legislation ottomane* (Istanbul: 1873–88); G. Young, *Corps de droit Ottoman* (Oxford: 1905–6).

11. A detailed account of these events, with some documents, is given in Cevdet Paşa, *Tezakir 1–12*, ed. Cavid Baysun (Ankara: 1953), pp. 101–152. Additional information may be found in the contemporary reports of the British acting vice-consul in Jedda, Stephen Page (F.O. 195/375). For a discussion, see William Ochsenwald, "Muslim European conflict in the Hijaz: the Slave Trade controversy, 1840–1859," *Middle Eastern Studies*, vol. 16 (1980): 115–126; and idem, *Religion, Society and the State in Arabia: the Hijaz under Ottoman control, 1840–1908* (Columbus, Ohio: 1984), pp. 117–127 and 138–141.

12. Cevdet, *Tezakir*, p. 111.

13. Cevdet, *Tezakir*, p. 133.

14. Cevdet, *Tezakir*, pp. 67–68.

15. See pp. 64–65 and 66–76.

16. See *EI²*, *s.v.* "Ḳurrat al-'Ayn. See also Farah Azari, ed., *Women of Iran: The Conflict with Fundamentalist Islam* (London: 1983), Chapter 5, by Sima Bahar; and Lois Beck and Nikki Keddie, eds., *Women in the Muslim World* (Cambridge, Mass.: 1978), especially Chapter 15, "Women and the Revolution in Iran, 1905–1911," by Mangol Bayat-Philipp.

17. W. Morgan Shuster, *The Strangling of Persia* (New York: 1912), [reprinted Washington, D.C., 1987], pp. 191–2.

CHAPTER 5

1. Josephus, *Contra Apionem*, II, 165.

2. On this see by A. K. Wensinck, "The Refused Dignity," in *A Volume of Oriental Studies Presented to Edward G. Browne, on his Sixtieth Birthday*, edited by T.W. Arnold and R.A. Nicholson (Cambridge: 1922), pp. 491–499.

3. On this point see B. Lewis, "The Significance of Heresy in Islam," *Studia Islamica* (1952): 43–63; reprinted in idem, *Islam in History*, pp. 275–294.

4. Ibn Qutayba, *'Uyūn al-Akhbār*, vol. 1 (Cairo: 1963), p. 2. English translation by Josef Horovitz, *Islamic Culture* (April: 1930), p. 185.

5. By a portentous ambiguity, the Arabic word *Khalīfa*, from which Caliph is derived, combines the two meanings.

6. See B. Lewis, "The Impact of the French Revolution on Turkey: Some Notes on the Transmission of Ideas," *Cahiers d'histoire mondiale*, vol. 1 (July 1953): 105–125. For discussions of secularism in the modern Islamic world see Niyazi Berkes, *The Development of Secularism in Turkey* (Montreal: 1964); Bassam Tibi, "Islam and Secularization," *Proceedings of the First International Islamic Philosophy Conference 19–22 November 1979: Cairo (Egypt)* (Cairo:1982), 65–79; and Fouad Zakariya, *Laïcité ou Islamisme: Les Arabes à l'heure du choix* (Paris-Cairo: 1991).

7. For a discussion of this literature, see Johannes J. G. Jansen, *The Dual Nature of Islamic Fundamentalism* (London: 1997).

8. *Al-Jihād: al-Farīḍa al-Ghā'iba*, n.p., n.d. (ca. 1982?) On this work and its author, see Johannes J. G. Jansen, *The Neglected Duty: The Creed of Sadat's Assassins and Islamic Resurgence in the Middle East* (New York and London: 1986), especially Chapter 1.

9. From time to time attempts were made by religious or political authorities to identify and extirpate incorrect beliefs and practices. But these are rare and atypical, and never amounted to an organized and established institution like the Holy Office. For examples, see *EI*² s.v. "Miḥna." Probably the closest approximation in Islamic history occurred in the Ottoman Empire in the sixteenth century. See Halil Inalcık, *The Ottoman Empire: The Classical Age 1300–1600* (London: 1973), Chapter 18, "The Triumph of Fanaticism," pp. 179 ff.

10. *Masīr-i Ṭālibī yā Sefarnāma-i Mīrzā Abū Ṭālib Khān*, ed. H. Khadīv-Jam (Tehran: 1974), pp. 250–1; cf. English trans. C. Stewart, *Travels of Mirza Abu Talib Khan . . .* (London: 1814), vol. 2, p. 81.

CHAPTER 6

1. *The Turkish Letters of Ogier Ghiselin de Busbecq*, translated by E. S. Forster (Oxford: 1927), pp. 19–21.

2. Ibid, p. 135.

3. John Evelyn, *The Diary*, vol. IV, ed. E.S. de Beer (London: 1955), p. 358; cit. Otto Kurz, *European Clocks and Watches in the Near East* (London-Leiden: 1975), p. 63.

4. Edward William Lane, *An Account of the Manners and Customs of the Modern Egyptians*, 5th ed., vol. II (London: 1871), p. 325.

5. Inscriptions in *Répertoire Chronologìque d'Epigraphie arabe*, vol. I (Cairo: 1931), pp. 13–16. Significantly, Jerusalem is still designated on these milestones by its Roman name, Aelia.

6. Jean Chesneau, *Le voyage de Monsieur d'Aramon*, ed. Ch. Schefer (Paris: 1887), pp. 17, 202; cit. Kurz, p. 24, note 2.

7. Fatima Müge Göçek, *Rise of the Bourgeoisie, Demise of Empire: Ottoman Westernization and Social Change*, p. 106. On the export of clocks from Europe, see David E. Landes, *Revolution in Time: Clocks and the Making of the Modern World* (Cambridge, Mass.: 1983), especially pp. 99ff.

8. Jāmī, *Salāmān va-Absāl* (Tehran: 1306 solar), p. 36; English translation in A. J. Arberry, *Fitzgerald's Salaman and Absal* (Cambridge: 1956), p. 146.

9. Kurz, pp. 86–86.

10. The Turkish text, from a document in the Istanbul archives, is given by E. Z. Karal, *Fransa-Mısır ve Osmanlı İmparatorluğu (1797–180)* (Istanbul: 1940), p. 108; the Arabic text as brought to Acre by Sir Sidney Smith, is given in an Arabic biography of Jazzar Pasha, (British Museum manuscript Oriental 3033, folio 48a) cf. *Ta'rīkh Aḥmad Bāshā* (Beirut: 1055), p. 125. There is some variation between the two.

11. Georges Duhamel, *Consultation au Pays d'Islam* (Paris: 1947), pp. 27–28.

CHAPTER 7

1. Adolphus Slade, *Record of Travels in Turkey, Greece &c. and of a Cruise in the Black Sea, with the Capitan Pasha, in the Years 1829, 1820, and 1831*, vol. i (London: 1833), pp. 135–6.

2. See E. de Leone, *L'Impero Ottomano nel primo periodo delle riforme (Tanzimat) secondo fonti italiani* (Milan: 1967), pp. 58–59, citing Cesare Vimercati, *Constantinopoli e l'Egitto* (Parato: 1849), p. 65.

3. Qazvīnī, *Kitāb Āthār al-Bilād*, ed. F. Wüstenfeld (Göttingen: 1848), h. 404.

4. For a fuller discussion, see B. Lewis, *The Muslim Discovery of Europe* (New York: 1982), pp. 262–274.

5. Princess Musbah Haidar, *Arabesque*, rev. ed. (London: 1968), p. 61.

6. Idem., pp. 178–9.

7. See *La première histoire de France en ture ottoman: Chronique des padichahs de France, 1572*, edit. and trans. Jean-Louis Bacqué-Grammont (Paris-Istanbul: 1997).

8. Manuscript in Egyptian National Library, History, no. 435.

9. See *Encyclopædia of Islam*, 2nd edition, *s.v.* "Maṭbaʿa," where further references are given. For studies on some special aspects see *The Introduction of the Printing Press in the Middle East; Culture and History*, vol. 16 (Oslo: 1997).

10. Kemal Atatürk, *Milli Eğitim Söylevleri*, Ankara I, pp. 29–30. English translation in B. Lewis, *The Emergence of Modern Turkey*, p. 274.

11. For a remarkable example see Samir al-Khalil, *The Monument: Art, Vulgarity and Responsibility in Iraq* (Berkeley-Los Angeles: 1991).

12. On artistic and architectural Westernization see Günsel Renda, "Europe and the Ottomans," in *Europa und die Kunst des Islam 15. bis 18. Jahrhundert*, XXV. Internationaler Kongress für Kunstgeschichte (Vienna: 1983), pp. 9–32.

CONCLUSION

1. This view was not shared by Ibn Khaldūn (1332–1406), generally recognized as the greatest of Arab historians. For him, the coming of the Turks was a manifestation of God's beneficent concern for the Muslims, and brought them strength and renewal at a time of weakness and decadence. Ibn Khaldūn, *Kitab al-ʿIbar*, vol. v, (Bulaq: 1284/1867), p. 371; translation in B. Lewis, ed., *Islam from the Prophet Muhammad to the Capture of Constantinople*, vol. I (New York: 1974), pp. 96–99.

2. Ahmed Zéki Pacha, "Une seconde tentative des Musulmans pour découvrir l'Amérique," *Bulletin de l'Institut d'Egypte*, vol. 2 (Cairo: 1920), pp. 57–9.

3. On a pioneer group of ideological Westernizers in Turkey see M. Şükrü Hanioğlu, "Garbcılar: their attitudes towards religion and their impact on the official ideology of the Turkish Republic," *Studia Islamica* (1997/2): 133–158.

4. See *EI²* svv "ʿAdjala" and "Araba" (on carts) and "Bārūd" (on firearms and artillery); for fuller discussions, see Rhoads Murphey, *Ottoman Warfare: 1500–1700* (London: 1999); and Richard W. Bulliet, *The Camel and the Wheel* (Cambridge, Mass.: 1975). For an example of the modern impact of wheels, see Donald Quataert, *Social Disintegration and Popular Resistance in the Ottoman Empire, 1881–1908: Reactions to European Economic Penetration* (New York: 1983), Chapter 4, "Working on the Anatolian Railway."

5. For some observations by one of the most perceptive of Western travelers, see Volney, *Voyage en Égypte et en Syrie*, ed. Jean Gaulmier (Paris-The Hague: 1959), especially p. 382.

Index